"Praise" for *How to Win a Fight with a Liberal*

Listen to what the critics *aren't* saying:

"The best way to win a fight with a liberal is to strap him to the roof of your car. The second best way is to use this book."

—*Mitt Romney*

"This book should be banned in all 57 states."

—*Barack Obama*

"This book will make the oceans rise with the tears of polar bears."

—*Al Gore*

"If this book were just a little fatter, I would hit on it."

—*Bill Clinton*

"For conservatives, the nine most terrifying words in the English language are: 'I'm from the government, and I'm here to help.' For liberals, the other 30,000 most terrifying words are contained in this book."

—*ghost of Ronald Reagan*

"This book should be required reading for everyone who wants to live on my moon colony."

—Newt Gingrich

"If Herman Cain were president, this book would only cost $9.99."

—Herman Cain

"I stand firmly against this package of lies about liberals and how to beat them. I can say with certitude that junk like this should be yanked off the shelves."

—Anthony Weiner

"When I started reading this book, I couldn't take my eyes off it. No seriously, I can't move my eyes or my face."

—Nancy Pelosi

"Hey, Barack, have you seen this book? It's a big f**king deal! Oh s**t, is this mic on?"

—Joe Biden

HOW TO
WIN A
FIGHT WITH A
LIBERAL

BY DANIEL KURTZMAN
www.FightLiberals.com

sourcebooks

Published by Sourcebooks, Inc.
P.O. Box 4410, Naperville, Illinois 60567-4410
(630) 961-3900
Fax: (630) 961-2168
sourcebooks.com

Library of Congress Cataloging-in-Publication Data

Kurtzman, Daniel.
  How to win a fight with a liberal / by Daniel Kurtzman.
    p. cm.
  (alk. paper)
  1. Liberalism—United States—Humor. I. Title.
  PN6231.L47K873 2012
  320.51'30973—dc23

                    2012007574

Printed and bound in Canada.
POD 10 9 8 7 6 5 4 3

Dedication

Contents

Introduction

"Many are asking if our political discourse has gotten too heated. And those people should go to hell!"

—**Stephen Colbert**

Have you ever become so infuriated while arguing with a raving liberal moonbat that you've seriously considered "occupying" his mouth with your fist?

How many times have you listened to the delusional rantings of an obnoxious colleague, loudmouthed uncle, or neighborhood blowhard while fantasizing about delivering the verbal smackdown they so richly deserve?

Or perhaps you've already called Homeland Security

to report your liberal opponent as an enemy combatant and volunteered your waterboarding services.

We've all been there—butting heads with some half-wit who refuses to submit to the inevitable wisdom of our political views. Whether you're a conservative, Republican, Tea Partier, libertarian, independent, or someone who's just tired of liberals and their idiocy, chances are those lefties have made you mad as hell, and since you picked up this book, you probably can't take it anymore.

But if you're like most people, your past attempts at butting heads with liberals have probably gone one of two ways: (1) you've tried reasoning with them, only to walk away with that throbbing pain that comes from banging your head against a wall of stupid; or (2) you've tried screaming at liberals, only to make yourself hoarse while they go about their business of picking your pocket and redistributing your wealth into the nearest compost pile.

Either way, who could blame you if you've decided that arguing with liberals is a hopeless cause? You probably figure it's best to simply avoid them, just as you would a crazy person ranting on a street corner (because sometimes it's better to leave Al Sharpton alone with his thoughts).

But unfortunately, that's part of the problem with political discourse in America today. Too many reasonable people shy away from debate and let their more determined and vocal left-wing rivals spew their nonsense with impunity. Left unchallenged, it then spreads across the political landscape like herpes. Soon it's everywhere—flaring up at neighborhood barbecues, encroaching upon you at the office water cooler, or, when you're least expecting it, creeping into your Facebook news feed.

By continuing to stay silent, you let them win. That's why if you want to defeat the Left, you must confront your enemies wherever they lurk and be prepared to rip them a new reality.

We won't lie to you. Beating liberals into submission is a tall order, especially in this political climate, where so many have insulated themselves in such airtight ideological cocoons that no inconvenient fact or droplet of common sense can penetrate it. It's like the Fort Knox of willful ignorance.

So what's an honest, liberal-loathing American to do?

The answer is to fight them with laughter. That's where this book comes in handy. We're not talking about turning political debate into a joke or making a mockery of serious issues. It's about learning how to wield humor as a weapon, cultivate your sense of irony, and sharpen your arguments with witty retorts. It's about learning to lighten things up as a way to maintain your own sanity and disarm your opponents.

Mark Twain once said, "The human race has one really effective weapon, and that is laughter." It's especially true in political debate. Just think of one of the most effective lines ever used in a presidential debate, when Ronald Reagan was asked during his 1984 face-off with Walter Mondale if his advanced age was a liability. "I want you to know that also I will not make age an issue of this campaign," Reagan said. "I am not going to exploit, for political purposes, my opponent's youth and inexperience."

In addition to helping you wage comedic warfare, this book also offers other handy tips that will help you outwit, out-mock, and outrage your liberal rivals. We will show you how to:

- ✮ Learn basic rules of engagement, including how to frame arguments to your advantage, point out hypocrisy, and properly ridicule your opponents when necessary.
- ✮ Throw winning comebacks at mindless Obama

lovers, tax-and-spend ignoramuses, and other purveyors of liberal nonsense.

★ Determine if you suffer from argumentile dysfunction and, if so, learn how to avoid deadly pitfalls, such as promoting conspiracy theories, using Nazi analogies, or making the mistake of arguing with idiots.

★ Identify bullshit arguments, slice through Swisscheese logic, and expose fallacious reasoning.

★ Survive family sparring matches, manage workplace squabbles, and even learn to cope if you're sleeping with the enemy.

★ Entertain your friends and terrify your enemies while arguing politics on Facebook and Twitter.

★ Use liberals' own words and deeds against them with the help of a handy guide to some of the most ridiculous, moronic, and laughable things today's liberal icons have said and done.

★ Should all else fail, hurl imaginative insults at your unmedicated, un-American opponents by selecting from a handy cheat sheet containing 125,000 winning putdowns.

Politics was never meant to be a spectator sport. Political debate is simply too important to be left to the so-called experts in Washington and the media, who invariably just screw it up for the rest of us. That's why it falls on ordinary citizens like you to take the fight to the Left and defend America against all the godless, bongo-playing, gun-grabbing, tax-hiking, granny-euthanizing, park-occupying, shower-avoiding socialists and the ideals for which they stand.

If you don't, the moonbats have already won.

CHAPTER 1

What It Means to Be a Conservative

"I never use the words Democrats and Republicans. It's liberals and Americans."

—James Watt, Interior Secretary
under Ronald Reagan

There's a reason twice as many Americans identify themselves as "conservative" as opposed to "liberal." Would you rather associate yourself with an ideology that is synonymous with patriotism, strength, freedom, family values, moral clarity, and making an honest living? Or would you rather align yourself with defeatism, elitism, permissive values, moral uncertainty, and government dependence—or as it's more commonly known, liberalism?

It's not a shocker that many Americans have come to view the partisan divide in those terms. While liberals were busy spreading misery in the Carter years, doom and gloom during the Reagan and H. W. Bush years, venereal diseases during the Clinton years, bitter divisiveness during the W. Bush years, and socialism in the Obama years, conservatives were busy conquering communism, fighting terrorism, reforming government, reining in the welfare state, and putting cold cash back in the hands of tax-weary Americans.

The conservative philosophy has always been simple: get government out of our lives and off our backs; promote individual liberty and personal responsibility; trust in the American people to power the free market and make our economy thrive; stop punishing success and rewarding failure; and never—no matter how badly elitist Democrats and their friends in the liberal media, Hollywood, or the United Nations demand it—apologize for America.

Of course, conservatives also have to contend with pesky things called elections. They've had their victories in recent years, but have also taken a few drubbings at the ballot box (the scar that is the Obama election is still throbbing). But when Republicans lose, it's usually a result of backing away from conservative principles; they don't cut spending enough, they don't do enough to rein in government, they don't blow up as many terrorists as the war plans called for, and they get punished.

In short, conservatives get hosed any time they forget who they are and what they stand for. You can't be persuasive if you buckle in the face of opposition. That goes for elected Republican officials and your average conservative on the street, too.

That's why, as a first step in girding for battle with liberals, it's essential to have a firm fix on your own beliefs. Take the following quiz to determine where you fit in the larger conservative mix.

 What Breed of Conservative Are You?

Choose the answers that most closely match your ideological leanings.

---

1. Which bumper sticker would you most likely put on your car?

___A. If You're Gonna Burn Our Flag, Wrap Yourself In It First

___B. Honk If I'm Paying Your Mortgage

_____C. I'll Keep My Guns, Freedom, And Money. You Can Keep The "Change."

_____D. In Case Of Rapture, This Car Will Be Unmanned

_____E. Another Former Fetus For Life

_____F. I'd Rather Be Waterboarding

2. If the Founding Fathers were alive today, they would be most appalled by which of the following?

_____A. President Obama's inexplicable need to bow to every world leader

_____B. Democrats' failure to see that the problem with socialism is that eventually you run out of other people's money

_____C. That a Kenyan-born Muslim stole a presidential election

_____D. That schools can teach our kids about condoms and clean needles but learning about Jesus is taboo

_____E. Reality TV

_____F. The blame-America-first crowd that doesn't know how to wage war on exploding underpants

3. An asteroid is headed for Earth. You have a seat on the last shuttle off the planet. If you could bring only one book with which to build a future civilization, what would it be?

_____A. *Patriots and Pinheads*, by Bill O'Reilly

_____B. *The Wealth of Nations*, by Adam Smith

_____C. *Atlas Shrugged,* by Ayn Rand

_____D. *The Bible*

_____E. *Going Rogue*, by Sarah Palin

_____F. *The Art of War*, by Sun Tzu

4. A second civil war has just broken out in America. Who is to blame?

_____A. Barack Obama—for issuing an executive order to outlaw handguns and raise taxes on Coors Light

_____B. Tax-and-spend liberals—for taking the "free" out of the free market and the "capital" out of capitalism

_____C. Liberal socialists—for attempting to create a government of, by, and for gay Marxist Muslim illegal immigrants

_____D. Bible-bashing secularists—for trying to ban God and for provoking His wrath

_____E. Planned Parenthood proponents—for encouraging our young people to fornicate like rabbits on Ecstasy, all in the name of so-called "public health"

_____F.   Liberal terrorist appeasers—for letting America's guard down and planning to respond to the next terror attack with a strongly worded letter

5. If you could time-travel to any historical event and bring one thing with you, what would you choose?

_____A.   The day of Obama's birth in Kenya—with a video camera

_____B.   The beginning of the 1990s bull market—with today's stock quotes

_____C.   Ronald Reagan's inauguration—with a cloning device

_____D.   The day _Roe vs. Wade_ was decided—with Chief Justice John Roberts

_____E.   The Palin/Bachmann inauguration—with confetti

_____F.   September 10, 2001—with a no-fly list

6. If you were a candidate for political office, what would your theme song be?

_____A.   "Made in America," by Toby Keith

_____B.   "Money (That's What I Want)," by The Beatles

_____C.   "Won't Get Fooled Again," by The Who

___D. "Spirit in the Sky," by Norman Greenbaum

___E. "I'd Do Anything for Love (But I Won't Do That)," by Meat Loaf

___F. "America, F**k Yeah" —theme song from *Team America: World Police*

7. You have a hot date with Ann Coulter, and she asks you to bring over dinner and a movie. What do you bring?

___A. Cheeseburgers, Freedom Fries, and *Red Dawn* with Patrick Swayze

___B. Filet mignon, champagne, and *Wall Street* with Michael Douglas

___C. Freshly hunted venison, Budweiser, and *Forrest Gump* with Tom Hanks

___D. Fish, wine, and *The Ten Commandments* with Charlton Heston

___F. Chicken-fried steak, eggs, and *The Undefeated* with Sarah Palin

___G. U.S. military MREs, sodium pentothal, and *300*

8. What region of the country would you most like to see kicked out of the Union?

___A. The Northeast—home to America-blaming apologists and ivory-tower-dwelling elitists

_____B. Inner cities—home to deadbeat crackheads and social welfare parasites

_____C. Washington, D.C.—home to incompetent crooks and liars who have usurped power from the people

_____D. The Left Coast—home to religion-bashing, tree-hugging sodomites and sinners

_____E. Hollywood—home to culture-perverting, values-defiling celebricrats

_____F. All the blue states—home to spineless, sushi-eating, terrorist-coddling, freedom-hating socialists who'd be happier living in France

9. If you could issue an executive order, which of the following would you most like to see happen?

_____A. Ban all automated phone systems that make you push "1" for English

_____B. Ban government bailouts and Marxist take-overs of major corporations

_____C. Require all presidential candidates to produce a valid birth certificate proving they are natural-born citizens

_____D. Require all government buildings to display

the Ten Commandments, and have all government officials follow them

_____E. Ban marriage between any same-sex persons, places, or things

_____F. Make it legal to detain anyone with a Muslim-sounding name and strip-search them for underwear bombs before boarding any plane, including Air Force One

10. If you could chisel any Americans, living or dead, onto Mt. Rushmore, who would you choose?

_____A. Dale Earnhardt, Johnny Cash, Chuck Norris, and Hank Williams Jr.

_____B. Exxon Mobil, Goldman Sachs, Halliburton, and Koch Industries (corporations are people too!)

_____C. Rush Limbaugh, Sean Hannity, Ann Coulter, and Glenn Beck

_____D. Revs. James Dobson, Rick Warren, Joel Osteen, and Carrie Prejean

_____E. Mike Huckabee, Michele Bachmann, Bill Bennett, and Phyllis Schlafly

_____F. Ronald Reagan, Dick Cheney, George W. Bush, and Jack Bauer

SCORING

If you answered mostly A's, you're a *Flag-waving Everyman*, also known as a patriot. You believe in championing liberty over tyranny, apple pie over sushi, and that God gave us a two-day weekend so we could enjoy football and NASCAR.

If you answered mostly B's, you're a *Free Marketeer*, also known as a fiscal conservative. You believe in free-market capitalism, tax cuts, and protecting your hard-earned cash from pickpocketing liberal socialists.

If you answered mostly C's, you're an *Anti-government Gunslinger*, also known as a libertarian conservative or Tea Partier. You believe in smaller government, states' rights, gun rights, and that, as Reagan once said, "The nine most terrifying words in the English language are, 'I'm from the government and I'm here to help.'"

If you answered mostly D's, you're a *Faith-based Fighter*, also known as a religious conservative. You believe in Judeo-Christian values, restoring God's rightful place in the public square, and in showing all the unwashed and unsaved liberal sinners the path to salvation, or at least to the GOP.

If you answered mostly E's, you're a *Values Guardian*, also known as a cultural conservative. You believe in protecting the American way of life and fighting a culture war against permissive liberals and the lapdogs in the lamestream media who are out to destroy decent, moral Americans like Sarah Palin and Michele Bachmann for daring to defend traditional values.

If you answered mostly F's, you're a *Freedom Crusader*, also known as a neoconservative. You believe in taking the fight directly to the enemy, whether it's terrorists abroad or the liberal terrorist appeasers at home who give them aid and comfort.

If your answers don't match any of the above, that means you're a label-defying iconoclast or a hybrid of various types. Consider it a point of pride.

If manual scoring is too antiquated for your tastes, you can take an online version of this quiz at www.FightLiberals .com, where you can also share your results with a friend.

"*If you don't stand for anything, you don't stand for anything!*"

—George W. Bush

As you can see, conservatives are a diverse breed. But there is a core set of values and common causes that unites them all. Since it's important to have a clear idea of your worldview before you engage liberals and go about the business of destroying theirs, we present…

The Conservative Manifesto

Conservatives believe in personal freedom, self-reliance, limited government, free enterprise, and defending America from those who would seek to turn it into a socialist nanny state.

Conservatives believe, as Ronald Reagan once said, that every day is the Fourth of July, while liberals believe that every day is April 15. (Or possibly 4/20.)

Conservatives believe in a shining city on a hill, and in protecting that shining city from terrorists, illegal aliens, and dirty drum-playing Occupiers.

Conservatives believe that if you're a lazy liberal hippie whiner and you want to "occupy" something, try a job.

Conservatives believe open-heart surgery, cancer treatment, and laparoscopic procedures shouldn't be run by the same people who brought you Fannie Mae, the IRS, and the DMV.

Conservatives believe that you will have to pry not just their guns, but their hard-earned money, their Bibles, and their incandescent light bulbs from their cold dead hands.

Conservatives believe any time is a good time to cut taxes, because the government thinks any time is a good time to waste your money on social services for freeloaders and foreign aid for Asscrackistan.

Conservatives believe that abortion should be considered murder, and not a government-sanctioned form of birth control that you can get at the drive-thru.

Conservatives believe Priuses are shaped that way so they can pass easily under your truck.

Conservatives believe if there are increases in the Earth's temperature, they can be directly attributed to CO_2 emissions from Al Gore.

Conservatives believe if rising oceans will flood the planet, you're going to need a bad-ass SUV to get around.

Conservatives believe "community organizer" is something you put on your résumé to hide the fact that you didn't have a real job.

Conservatives believe a health-care policy is like a new car: everyone should be able to buy one, just don't ask them to pay for yours.

Conservatives believe there isn't always a cop around when you need one, but a Colt .45 is always on the job, which is why they also believe the only waiting period in gun ownership should be the time it takes to reload.

Conservatives believe in enhanced interrogation,

including waterboarding, because it's easier to ask for forgiveness than it is to clean up fallen towers, bodies, and rubble.

Conservatives believe that there ought to be a constitutional amendment requiring that every liberal who threatens to move to Canada any time a Republican gets elected president actually has to move to Canada.

Conservatives believe in God, faith, and family, and that listening to Hollywood liberals talk about values is like listening to the French talk about military deterrence.

Conservatives believe that any elected Democrat who apologizes for America, undermines our values, and gives aid and comfort to our enemies ought to be sent to Gitmo to serve out the remainder of his or her term.

Conservatives believe that if Washington is the answer, then the question must be ridiculous.

And above all, conservatives have unwavering faith in the strength and character of the American people and every confidence that our great nation will triumph in the struggle over the twin evils of our time— terrorism and liberalism.

Rate Your Partisan Intensity Quotient (PIQ)

Beyond basic ideology, we also need to assess your partisan temperament. Are you the type of person who eagerly engages liberals in debate, or do you avoid confrontation at all costs? Answer the following questions, and we'll rate your PIQ.

1. Your neighbor has just placed a very large Obama 2012 sign on her lawn. Which of the following would you do?

____A. Show respect for her right to free speech

____B. Put up an even larger Romney 2012 sign

____C. Graffiti her sign in the middle of the night by writing "Sucks" underneath "Obama"

____D. Graffiti your own Romney 2012 sign and then publicly accuse her of defacing your property

2. You're stuck in a traffic jam created by "Occupy" protesters blocking an intersection. Which of the following would you do?

____A. Sit in your car patiently while the police clear the street

_____B. Blast Rush Limbaugh on the radio to drown out their chanting

_____C. Send the organizer a bouquet of flowers with a card that says, "Thanks for all your help xoxox, Al Qaeda"

_____D. Try to get through to NORAD to call in air strikes

3. You encounter a Greenpeace activist who is soliciting money outside a grocery story and asking you to sign his petition to ban oil exploration and drilling. Which of the following would you do?

_____A. Avoid eye contact and pretend you didn't hear or see him

_____B. Tell him thank you, but you believe energy independence is critical to American security, and drilling and exploration can be done safely

_____C. Tell him patchouli oil isn't deodorant and quit bothering people who actually have jobs

_____D. Give him repeated Heisman Trophy stiff arms while yelling, "Drill, baby, drill!"

4. You receive an email from HR that this year's office Christmas party will be replaced by a "Winter Holiday Party." Which of the following would you do?

_____A. Send a polite thank you to Human Resources and cancel the invitations you ordered

_____B. Forgive them for they know not what they do

_____C. Ignore the email and proceed with Secret Santa assignments

_____D. Construct a manger scene in the employee cafeteria

5. You're at your daughter's school and the chair of the PTA is demanding that homosexuality be added to the sex-ed curriculum. Which of the following would you do?

_____A. Suggest that homosexuality could be added if the parent is notified and could opt for his child not to attend

_____B. Pillage your retirement and enroll your children in a private school

_____C. Point out that he ought to be more concerned that American test scores are well behind those of South Korea, Canada, Finland, and a host of other countries

_____D. Let him know that kids learn plenty about homosexuality just by watching *Glee*

6. You're at a Republican campaign rally when you encounter a smelly hippie with multiple body piercings hoisting a sign that says "Jesus save us—from the Republicans." Which of the following would you do?

_____A. Embrace him in the spirit of brotherly love

_____B. Move to another part of the crowd to avoid a confrontation

_____C. Hoist up your own sign to block him from the cameras and the podium

_____D. Wrestle him to the ground and smack him repeatedly with your Bible

7. You're at a family barbecue and your unemployed brother-in-law starts ranting about the need for even more government spending to create jobs. Which of the following would you do?

_____A. Play *Angry Birds* on your iPhone to take out your aggressions

_____B. Say a quiet prayer for your sister to get divorced

_____C. Tell him that until government gets out of the

way and stops choking the economy, the only jobs that are going to be created are in the unemployment office

____D. Teach his kids how to write IOUs in crayon and when they ask why, tell them, "Because daddy mortgaged your future"

8. You've just been given the opportunity to meet Barack Obama face-to-face. Which of the following would you do?

____A. Tell him what an honor it is to meet him

____B. Think about what a spineless liberal he is but hold your tongue out of respect

____C. Ask him why we should give him a second term when he whiffed so badly during his first four-year debacle

____D. Say "Boo" and watch him cower and wet himself like he usually does when confronted by Republicans

Scoring Your PIQ

Award yourself zero points for every A, one point for every B, two points for every C, and three points for every D.

20–24: Severe ☆☆☆☆☆☆☆☆☆☆☆☆☆☆☆

You're a *Flame-Throwing Revolutionary*: There's a water-board and an "enemy combatant" label in your future, and it may help if you're not allergic to tear gas.

15–19: High ☆☆☆☆☆☆☆☆☆☆☆☆☆

You're a *Fierce Fighter*. You will argue politics any time and any place, which makes you unpopular at funerals, weddings, and baby showers.

10–14: Elevated ☆☆☆☆☆☆☆

You're a *Passionate Foot Soldier*. You stand up for what you believe in, but odds are, like most people, you'll bail out of an argument if things get heated.

5–9: Guarded ☆☆☆

You're a *Casual Observer*. You speak up when you feel it's safe, but not if it conflicts with *NCIS*.

0–4: Low ☆

You're a *Noncombatant*. You're like the French of political discourse, waving the white flag at the slightest sign of resistance. Time to grow a pair.

What's Your State of Embattlement?

Everyone is familiar with the much-ballyhooed red vs. blue divide, which separates America into Republican and Democratic states. But that obviously doesn't tell the whole story, as no state is uniformly red or blue. You've heard of other regional divides like the Bible Belt and the Rust Belt, but there are many other "belts" that describe partisan America. To determine your state of embattlement, locate the belt below that most closely corresponds to your specific locality.

THE BELTS OF BLUE AMERICA

If you are a conservative living in…

The Born-This-Way Belt (enclaves of America that are fabulously gay)

The Botox Belt (the land of high cheekbones, fake boobs, and liposuctioned fannies, from Hollywood to Manhattan)

The Bagel Belt (urban areas with a high concentration of equal parts wisecracking and complaining Jews: "You call this soup hot? Feh!")

The Ivory-Tower Belt (cocoons dominated by intellectual and academic elites)

The Tofurky Belt (the land of militant vegans and hairy, naked tree-huggers)

The Bong Belt (stoner country, where the munchies dictate day-to-day activities)

…you are *Desperately Besieged*. You're surrounded by so many liberals, it's like being the last person left at the end of a zombie movie. Arguing with them seems like a lost cause, and the best you can do is lay low and hide, lest they suck out your brain and turn you into one of them. Remember the shoot-out at the end of *Butch Cassidy and the Sundance Kid*? That's pretty much what you're looking at.

THE BELTS OF PURPLE AMERICA

If you are a conservative living in…

The Cookie-Cutter Belt (middle-class planned communities where you can't tell your house from your neighbor's house, also known as Oxycontin Country)

The Can't-Buckle-My-Belt (where fatties are furious over the shrinking American pie and the fact that it's not all-you-can-eat)

The Slot-Jockey Belt (casino country, where smoking, booze and one-armed bandits rule the land, e.g., Nevada, Atlantic City, Mississippi River Valley)

The Stroke Belt (retirement communities from Florida to Arizona, overrun by silver foxes)

The Kitsch Belt (small towns built around roadside kitsch and tourist schlock)

The Meth Belt (where rolling meth labs keep the burbs humming and dentists in business)

…you are *Battle-Hardened*. You have so many fights you want to pick with the liberals all around you that you may not even know where to start. Sleep with one eye open and make sure you know who your friends are.

THE BELTS OF RED AMERICA

If you are a conservative living in…

The Dow Jones Belt (where the belts they wear cost more than your house)

The Megachurch Belt (where come-as-you-are churches have grown so large they have their own zip codes)

The Chastity Belt (southern and middle America, where abstinence is all the rage)

The Caviar-and-Cocaine Belt (home to the old money, country-club set)

The Border Belt (the barn door of America, where people come and go as they please)

The Locked-and-Loaded Belt (shoot-first, ask-no-questions-later country)

…you are *Safely Entrenched*. You're surrounded by

so many people who agree with you that your arguing skills may have gone flabby from disuse. Be careful not to injure your neck from nodding in agreement.

Whatever situation you find yourself in, your goal is the same: engage your enemies wherever they lurk. But first you must understand your enemy…

CHAPTER 2

Know Your Enemy

"If you know the enemy and know yourself, you need not fear the result of a hundred battles. If you know yourself but not the enemy, for every victory gained you will also suffer a defeat."

—Sun Tzu, *The Art of War*

B efore you engage liberals in combat, it's important to have a clear understanding of exactly who your enemies are, including their core beliefs, specific ideological profile, and vision for America. Doing so will enable you to better dissect, ridicule, and exploit their weaknesses for maximum advantage.

For starters, here's a look at what liberals truly stand for:

The Liberal Manifesto

Liberals believe in endless tax hikes, cradle-to-grave welfare, class warfare, and that the best way to create jobs is to first go after all of the "evil" corporations that create them, which is like wanting to create oxygen by burning down all the trees.

Liberals believe it's evening in America, and they just proposed a kilowatt tax for keeping the lights on.

Liberals believe Starbucks and Planned Parenthood should merge because it would be more environmentally friendly if teenagers could get their Frappuccinos and abortions at the same drive-thru.

Liberals believe that technology like solar, wind, unicorn, and Wonder Twins power are viable substitutes for low-cost fossil fuels that actually work.

Liberals believe the best way to combat terrorism is through a stern series of United Nations-mandated "time-outs."

Liberals believe in unionized labor, unreasonable taxes, and unnecessary regulations, and then wonder why companies ship jobs overseas.

Liberals believe in turning lovely New York parks into recreations of Woodstock so they can drink booze, have sex, and whine in front of TV cameras.

Liberals believe they are the 99% and are willing to

"occupy" anything to prove it, except maybe a job or a shower stall.

Liberals believe that if you are a lazy, drunken, handout-seeking loser who complains about not being able to get a job—despite spending all day sitting on the couch eating Funyuns—everyone else is to blame but yourself.

Liberals believe in frivolous lawsuits and class actions, and you better not oppose them or they'll sue.

Liberals believe in government-run health care, because when you need brain surgery, why not trust the same people who brought you the tax code, FEMA, and the efficiency of the Post Office?

Liberals believe in environmentally protected mountain majesties, fruited plains of overpriced wind turbines, and amber waves of spotted owls, polar bears, and leprechauns.

Liberals believe in an ideology based on the idea that (1) government can make wiser decisions than individuals; (2) people shouldn't be forced to accept personal responsibility; and (3) "anything goes" when it comes to morality, especially if it involves Astroglide.

Liberals believe in taxing sin even though they don't believe in God.

Liberals believe the Ten Commandments shouldn't

be displayed in public places because they hope to get into heaven by pleading ignorance.

Liberals believe Obama was not born in Kenya, but in a manger in Jerusalem, and that he can heal the sick, feed the multitudes with five loaves of bread and two fish, make it rain $100 bills, and enact universal rainbows and ponies for everyone.

Liberals believe their values are as American as apple pie, even though they want the government to take that pie away from your children and replace it with a bowl of arugula from Michelle Obama's garden.

Liberals believe it's wrong to racially profile, but always lock the doors on their BMWs when driving through "urban" neighborhoods.

Liberals believe in giving amnesty to immigrants who broke the law and entered the country illegally—or as liberals like to call it, a "voter registration drive."

Liberals believe the polar ice caps are going to melt any day now and turn the Rocky Mountains into oceanfront property.

Liberals believe that if people want to marry their same-sex partner, their pet, their blow-up doll, or their cardboard cutout of Ryan Seacrest, that's their right as an American.

Liberals believe in legalizing drug use for everything

from weed to LSD to heroin, because it's the only way they can believe Al Franken was ever funny.

Liberals believe in taking away your money, your guns, your crucifix, and your non-vegetable-oil-fueled car.

Liberals believe Happy Meals and Jesus have no place in schools, but it's perfectly OK to teach kids to masturbate.

Liberals don't believe in the death penalty except in the case of an unborn fetus.

Liberals believe that singing songs, holding hands, waving candles, and holding up signs that read "Think peace" can solve all the world's problems.

Liberals believe that America's best days are behind us and that it's imperative to create new laws, taxes, and regulations to make sure they stay there.

Liberals believe that no matter how badly their policies destroy jobs and the economy, it's never too late to blame Bush.

And worst of all, liberals believe that your failure to share their belief in all of the above makes you a politically incorrect, intolerant, bigoted, uninformed, evil, stupid, fascist moron from "flyover country."

"The liberal is continually angry, as only a self-important man can be, with his civilization, his culture, his country, and his folks back home. His is an infantile world-view. At the core of a liberal is the spoiled child—miserable, as all spoiled children are, unsatisfied, demanding, ill-disciplined, despotic, and useless. Liberalism is a philosophy of sniveling brats."

—P. J. O'Rourke

Frequently Asked Questions About Liberals

Now that you know what you're up against, it's time to get to the vexing questions about liberals' peculiar behavior and seemingly inexplicable belief system.

Q. Why are liberals so damn angry all the time?

A. If you had elected a leader on the promise of hope and change, then discovered he was so inept he couldn't even sell cocaine to Charlie Sheen, watched your party leaders spend most of their time arguing with each other, and saw your very ideology turn into such a dirty word that you were embarrassed to even admit you were a liberal, the veins in your forehead would be perpetually throbbing too. Plus, no one wears deodorant at their rallies.

Q. Is there anything liberals consistently stand for?

A. To answer that, first you must pay a question tax.

Q. Why are liberals still blaming George W. Bush for the country's problems, four years into Obama's presidency?

A. Liberals are fixated with their version of the *Star Wars* myth in which Bush is Darth Vader and Dick Cheney is Emperor Palpatine, with Obama in the role of Luke Skywalker. The only problem is Barack Oskywalker really sucks at the Force. He can't levitate the economy and his socialist policies are bankrupting the Federation. Liberals just can't admit that the Force is not strong with this one. So like any spoiled child, all they can do is blame Anakin.

Q. Why do liberals hate success?

A. Liberalism is based on the Marxist ideology of the redistribution of wealth and the idea that business is the enemy. If you're successful you undoubtedly exploited workers, ravaged the environment, and killed puppies. So you must be punished for your success. After all, success breeds success, and if there are too many successful people, who would vote for liberals?

Q. Why do liberals hate America so much?

A. Liberals hate America because America stands for everything that liberals hate: Judeo-Christian values, personal responsibility, hard work, individual liberty, free markets, and winning. That's why they want to "fix" America to be more like France or Sweden so we can be a nation of do-nothing pot-smoking socialist bisexuals who can't hit a curveball.

Q. Why do liberals have such a hard time taking a simple stand on an issue? Why are they always for something one day, then against it the next?

A. No one really knows why, but some experts speculate that because they spend so much time holding their fingers to the wind, they don't get enough blood flow to their brains.

Q. Why are liberals so ignorant?

A. To quote Ronald Reagan, "The trouble with our liberal friends is not that they are ignorant, but that they know so much that isn't so."

"A Democrat sees the glass of water as half-full. A Republican looks at the same glass and wonders who the hell drank half his glass of water."

—**Comedian Jeff Cesario**

Q. Why are liberals so sanctimonious about the need for everyone to be politically correct, but find it perfectly okay to call Tea Party members "teabaggers"?

A. We know it sounds hypocritical, but remember when the boy or girl in your kindergarten class pulled your hair? Did that mean they hated you? Liberals have a secret crush on the Tea Party. The Tea Party is a young, hot, viable grassroots movement with a clearly defined ideology of low taxes and small government that's made up of the middle- and working-class people. The Tea Party has energy and idealistic zeal. Liberalism is the old, sagging, tarted-up vestige of a failed, dying belief system, so you can't blame them if they are a little jealous of the pretty new girl.

Q. Why are liberals so intellectually condescending?

A. Those who can, do. Those who can't, look down on the ones who are actually doing, and then look for ways to tax them.

Q. Are liberals evil?

A. No. But as Sean Hannity has aptly pointed out, they just have "a disturbing habit of winking at evil, of ignoring it, or turning a blind eye to it."

Q. Why is it so acceptable for liberals to lie for political ends?

A. You'll notice the only difference between "liberal" and "libel" is two letters.

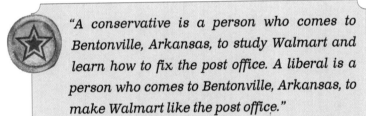

"A conservative is a person who comes to Bentonville, Arkansas, to study Walmart and learn how to fix the post office. A liberal is a person who comes to Bentonville, Arkansas, to make Walmart like the post office."

—Newt Gingrich

Q. Do all liberals endorse sexually permissive, deviant behavior?

A. It depends on what the meaning of the word "yes" is.

Q. How can anyone expect liberal Democrats to solve the nation's problems when all they do is whine and gripe? Do they even have a plan?

A. Democrats actually have a carefully thought-out,

multipronged approach to problem solving, consisting of the following steps: (1) conduct a focus group to identify a problem; (2) propose tax hikes as a solution; (3) accuse anyone who opposes said solution of intolerance; (4) conduct an opinion poll to gauge support; (5) reverse position; (6) debate themselves endlessly over whether they have, in fact, reversed position; (7) deny that the problem exists; (8) do nothing while Republicans fix the problem.

Q. Are there any similarities between liberals and conservatives?

A. To quote former House Majority Leader Dick Armey, "I said to my liberal friend that we are fundamentally the same. I spend money like it's my money and you spend money like it's my money."

Q. Liberals seem to take themselves way too seriously. Why won't they lighten up already?

A. Liberals are appalled that you would even ask that question at a time when glaciers need refreezing, wetlands need rewetting, deadbeat crackheads need handouts, unqualified minorities need guaranteed college admittance, and illegal immigrants need citizenship. Until then, everyone else must be made to suffer.

"Never underestimate the power of stupid people in large groups."

—Anonymous

A Field Guide to the Liberal Genus

Now it's time for you to meet the various species that make up the Democratic voting bloc. Familiarize yourself with this handy field guide so that you can quickly size up your opponent.

OCCUPY WALL GEEKS

Unemployed losers who spend their time blaming hard-working wealthy Americans for their own failure by taking over public parks, camping, smoking pot, and not bathing

A.k.a.: The proletariat, the 99%, philosophy majors

Natural habitat: Tents, youth hostels, Apple stores (with daddy's credit card)

Turn-ons: Blaming Wall Street, redistributing wealth, defecating in public places, using what was previously known as jazz hands or spirit fingers for group communication

Turn-offs: Success, private property, want ads, job interviews

Likely to be seen: Demanding institutional financial responsibility and corporate accountability

Would sooner be caught dead than: Being personally responsible or accountable

MADDOW-LANDERS

Tax-applauding, big-government-touting, Rachel Maddow-worshipping elites who believe that parroting sound bites from MSNBC while smirking constitutes an act of civil disobedience

A.k.a.: Latte liberals, limousine liberals, liberal elites

Natural habitat: Wealthy urban enclaves and posh suburbs, heavily concentrated in ivory towers, beach condos, and wine bars

Turn-ons: Nanny states, sushi, chardonnay, class warfare

Turn-offs: Fox News, the NRA, SUVs (except their own), bad feng shui, public displays of the Ten Commandments

Likely to be seen: Eating macrobiotic greens at a Willie Nelson benefit concert for the Barack Obama Legal Defense Fund

Would sooner be caught dead than: In church

GRANOLACRATS

Liberal environmental activists dedicated to the proposition that all men, spotted owls, and bean sprouts are created equal

A.k.a.: Tree-huggers, eco-wackos, enviro-mentals, eco-terrorists

Natural habitat: Small coastal cities, college towns, and suburbs with a suitable climate for growing cannabis

Turn-ons: Spotted owls, windmills, naked yoga, ozone, magic mushrooms, vandalizing SUVs

Turn-offs: Fossil fuels, common sense, deodorant, toilet paper containing less than 50 percent recycled fibers

Likely to be seen: Chastising patrons at the local food co-op who forget to bring their reusable bags

Would sooner be caught dead than: Eating food that is not organic, fair trade, cruelty-free, sustainably farmed, locally grown, hand-crafted, vegan, artisanal, and carbon neutral

KRUGMANOIDS

Smug Ivy League whack jobs and disciples of *New York Times* columnist Paul Krugman who want to fix the economy by doubling down on failed stimulus programs by taxing the rich, borrowing more money, then flushing it down the toilet with wasteful government spending programs

A.k.a: Keynesians, tax-and-spenders, pinko socialists

Natural habitat: Harvard faculty club, MSNBC green room, executive boards of failed green energy companies like Solyndra

Turn-ons: Entitlement programs, crony capitalism, double-digit unemployment

Turn-offs: Balanced budgets, fiscal responsibility, sanity

Likely to be seen: Writing a dissertation, blog, or column

Would sooner be caught dead than: Running a company or creating jobs

NUTROOTS

Loudmouthed lefties who are constantly looking to leverage the Internet and other new media to more efficiently spew their hatred of success, God, and America

A.k.a.: Lefty bloggers, Neterati, property of George Soros

Natural habitat: Their parents' basements

Turn-ons: Hyper-partisanship, left-wing propaganda, MoveOn.orgies

Turn-offs: Reason, individual success, rational thought

Likely to be seen: Cluttering your inbox with inflammatory lies while asking for more money to spread them

Would sooner be caught dead than: Listening to a dissenting opinion

OPPRESSEDBYTERIANS

Oppressed, left-wing agitators primarily concerned with social injustice, the suppression of minority rights, and more importantly, trying to make every friend, relative, or passerby feel guilty about it

A.k.a.: Disadvantaged Democrats, identity politics activists, PC police, feminazis, professional victims

Natural habitat: College campuses, inner cities, nonprofit organizations

Turn-ons: Political correctness, welfare, affirmative action, amnesty for illegals, gangsta rap

Turn-offs: "The man"

Likely to be seen: Berating you and recommending "sensitivity training" for using terms like "poor," "lazy," and "crackhead" rather than "economically marginalized," "motivationally challenged," and "artificial-stimulant victim"

Would sooner be caught dead than: Pledging allegiance to a non-rainbow flag

HOLLYWOOD IGNORATI

Politically active Hollywood liberals who believe everyone has an obligation to hear and affirm their glamorous, morally superior opinions

A.k.a.: Celebricrats, celiberals, Hollywood elites

Natural habitat: Gated hillside Malibu homes, posh Manhattan penthouses, rehab

Turn-ons: Ethiopian orphans, Versace, Kabbalah, orgies, shotgun divorces, juice fasting, drunk driving

Turn-offs: Everything else

Likely to be seen: Driving a stretch Hummer to their private jet after lecturing people about energy conservation

Would sooner be caught dead than: Accepting an award without first denouncing the Tea Party or corporate America

PETARDS

Animal-rights fanatics who believe meat is murder, rather than a tasty, delicious food group; that drug companies shouldn't try and cure cancer if it means testing on a bunny; and that chickens, pigs, and lobsters have the right to an attorney

A.k.a.: Friends of fur, animal rights activists, furverts

Natural habitat: Mall parking lots where they try to get you to sign one of their petitions

Turn-ons: Reminding you of how superior they are because they don't eat meat; showing you disgusting videos of slaughterhouses right before lunch

Turn-offs: People who wear fur, people who eat meat, people in general

Likely to be seen: Stepping over homeless people to protest Kim Kardashian, Super Mario, or KFC

Would sooner be caught dead than: Actually helping a human being

Other Liberal Species You May Encounter

OBAMESSIANICS
Fervent liberals who believe Barack Obama is the second coming of Jesus Christ

HILLARY KRISHNAS
Devout liberals who long to restore a Clintonian government with all of the liberal idealism and none of the fellatio

ALSHARPTONIANS
A specific set of Oppressedbyterians who play with a fifty-two-card deck composed entirely of race cards

ACL-EUNUCHS
Extremely voluble left-wing activists who can be heard whining and shrieking like impotent choir boys about disappearing civil liberties

COMMIEKAZIS

Left-wing pinko commies who rail against capitalism and believe America could achieve greatness if only it were Cuba

MARIJUANICANS

Weed-toking stoners who claim all the world's problems would be solved by legalizing marijuana, but whose political agenda is really just about taking the hassle out of getting pot

KUMBAYANIKS

Peace-loving, patchouli-oil-covered hippies who believe in ridiculously oversimplified slogans, not war

CONFLAGRATIONISTS

Radical, flag-burning anarchists who defecate on police cars, vandalize chain stores, and hurl garbage cans through Starbucks' windows (*after* buying their Grande Mocha Frappuccinos)

ATHE-IDIOTS

Atheists who don't believe in God and feel the need to impose their lack of belief on everyone around them by sucking the joy out of everything from Christmas to the Pledge of Allegiance

GLEEVANGELICALS

Urban professional sodomites whose rallying cry is "We're here, we're registered at Bloomingdales; get used to it."

"Hell is other people."

—Jean-Paul Sartre

How to Rate a Liberal's Partisan Intensity Quotient (PIQ)

In addition to being familiar with various liberal species, you will also need to gauge the extent of your opponent's partisan passion, inflexibility, or possible pathology. You can quickly determine your opponent's PIQ with this simple test. Award one point for each "yes" answer.

_____1. Do they begin more than half their sentences with "Well, in Europe…"

_____2. Do they own a copy of "The Communist Manifesto," *Quotations from Chairman*

Mao Tse-Tung, or anything written by Michael Moore?

_____3. Are they lobbying to replace mall Santas with guys dressed like Paul Krugman?

_____4. Do they go around boasting about how their carbon footprint is smaller than yours?

_____5. Instead of using a GPS, do they ask the universe for guidance?

_____6. When arguing, are the words "bro" or "dude" used for emphasis?

_____7. Are they convinced the world can run exclusively on solar energy, wind power, and a really intense spin class?

_____8. Are they for the legalization of marijuana solely because it will give the government something else to tax and regulate?

_____9. Instead of playing Mozart to their unborn children, do they play the Grateful Dead?

_____10. Do they think the cutoff for late-term abortion should be when a fetus graduates college?

_____11. Do they assign most of the world's problems to big business, Jesus, and *Celebrity Apprentice*?

_____12. Do they regard the *New York Times*, NPR, and MSNBC as part of a *right-wing* media conspiracy?

_____13. Do they refer to a steak house as a murder buffet?

_____14. Do they hate Christmas because of the low percentage of union membership among elves?

_____15. Does their family pet have a Native American name?

_____16. Do they attend $200-a-plate dinners to raise money for the hungry?

_____17. Do they cite *Planet of the Apes* as a reason to end testing on animals?

_____18. Do they post Facebook status updates that say, "97% of you won't mention the plight of the Peruvian giant toad, but those who do will really make a difference"?

_____19. Do they refer to the Bush presidency as a "regime," "crime syndicate," or "junta"?

_____20. Do they make fun of your Civil War reenactment on their way to a Star Trek convention?

SCORING

16–20: SEVERE

Your opponent is an *Unhinged Extremist*. Approach with extreme caution.

12–15: HIGH

Your opponent is a *Pugnacious Pitbull*. Nothing short of an absolute beatdown will give them pause for thought.

8–11: ELEVATED

Your opponent is a *Dedicated Disciple*. Wear a hard hat and pack a lunch.

4–7: GUARDED

Your opponent is a *Casual Combatant*. Overwhelm them with shock and awe.

0–3: LOW

Your opponent is a *Guaranteed Pushover*. This guy should fall faster than Barack Obama's approval ratings.

> *"The Democrats seem to be basically nicer people, but they have demonstrated time and again that they have the management skills of celery. They're the kind of people who'd stop to help you change a flat but would somehow manage to set your car on fire. I would be reluctant to entrust them with a Cuisinart, let alone the economy."*
>
> **—Dave Barry**

A Glimpse into the Liberal Utopia

Liberals are working hard to build a society that realizes their dreams for total domination over America's political and cultural landscape.

Whether they succeed or fail will depend on your commitment to derailing their plans. To illustrate what's at stake, here's a glimpse into America's possible future should liberals have their unfettered way with the country.

NEWSPAPER HEADLINES LIBERALS WOULD LOVE TO SEE

★ Revised, Politically Correct Pledge of Allegiance to Exclude God, America, Liberty, and Justice

★ U.S. Extends Social Security Benefits to Mexico

★ New Border Fence to Include Revolving Doors and Flashing Neon Sign that Says "Open"

★ Government Doubles Down on Green Energy with Billion-Dollar Subsidies for Magic Fairy Dust Production

★ New EPA and Labor Regulations Shut Down Santa's Sweatshop; North Pole to Close, Elves Laid Off

★ National Government Health-Care System Extends Benefits to Pets; Doggie Death Panels Set to Convene; Cats Lose Three of Nine Lives

★ Burka the New Black on Red Carpet as Sharia Law Sweeps Hollywood

★ New Government-mandated Abortion Policy Ensures "No Child Left Alive"

★ Dollars to Be Recycled as U.S. Currency No Longer Worth Paper Printed On.

★ Government Backs Plan for Power Plants Fueled by Raves, Ecstasy, and Gay Sex

- ★ Senate Democrats Pass Bill to Stomp Out Employment; Small Business Owners Added to Endangered Species List
- ★ PBS, *Sesame Street* Welcome New Pedophile Character "Feelie"
- ★ ACLU Wins! Religious Institutions Must Enforce Separation of Church and God
- ★ "Doggie-style" Outlawed as PETA Campaign Pays Off
- ★ Liberals Triumph in War on Christmas; Ed Bagley in Prius Replaces Santa on Sleigh
- ★ Gay Marriage Legalized; Hillary Clinton, Nancy Pelosi Wed in White House Rose Garden Ceremony
- ★ Liberals Request Brain-Eating Zombies Be Reclassified as "Undead Americans"
- ★ UFO Sighted, Liberals Offer Amnesty

Don't think it could ever happen? Well, no one ever thought a smooth-talking socialist with the middle name "Hussein" and a questionable country of origin would be president, but there you go. Not to put too much pressure on you, but if you don't do your part to help frustrate their plans, the liberal utopians will have won.

CHAPTER 3

Can't We All Just Get Along?

"As Americans, we must ask ourselves: Are we really so different? Must we stereotype those who disagree with us? Do we truly believe that ALL red-state residents are ignorant, racist, fascist, knuckle-dragging, NASCAR-obsessed, cousin-marrying, roadkill-eating, tobacco-juice-dribbling, gun-fondling, religious, fanatic rednecks; or that ALL blue-state residents are godless, unpatriotic, pierced-nose, Volvo-driving, France-loving, left-wing, communist, latte-sucking, tofu-chomping, holistic-wacko, neurotic, vegan, weenie perverts?"

—Dave Barry

L et's face it. Our great nation has been divided along fierce partisan lines ever since the days of our Founding Fathers, when even our finest powdered-wig-wearing, silk-stocking-strutting statesmen exchanged bitter recriminations over who was the bigger girlie-man.

With liberals and conservatives, Democrats and Republicans, and blue staters and red staters growing more polarized by the day, is there any hope left of finding common ground? The answer is yes. But before we get to that, let's first take stock of America's current state of disunion to discover exactly how deeply and ridiculously divided we have become.

A Day in the Life of Conservatives vs. Liberals

Conservatives and liberals may live in the same cities and breathe the same air, but they might as well be gliding along two separate planes of existence.

A Day in the Life of a Conservative	A Day in the Life of a Liberal
★ 7:00 a.m.	
Wake up, flip on Fox News, find out what to be afraid of today	Wake up, turn on MSNBC, find out what to be outraged by today
★ 8:00 a.m.	
Bible study	Home Bikram yoga
★ 8:30 a.m.	
Blare Rush Limbaugh while idling at McDonald's drive-through	Read *High Times* while sitting at a juice bar sipping wheat grass
★ 9:00 a.m.	
Arrive at work, secure rights to drill in ancient panda den	Arrive at work, begin sorting through frivolous lawsuits to prepare for filing
★ 10:00 a.m.	
Update Facebook with pictures from this week's NRA spotted-owl BBQ	Update Facebook with pictures from shamanic drum circle

A Day in the Life of a Conservative	A Day in the Life of a Liberal
★ 11:00 a.m.	
Log on to the *Drudge Report* to read about latest terrorist threat involving gay illegal immigrants posing as abortion doctors	Log on to the *Huffington Post* to read about Republican plans to build waterboarding theme park on National Mall
★ 12:00 p.m.	
Eat half a deer burger (left over from weekend hunt), wash down with Bud, throw the rest away	Cleansing fast! No lunch today
★ 1:00 p.m.	
Buy 100-share lot of Halliburton stock in anticipation of war with Iran	Buy solar-powered laptop case to offset guilt for racing against a Prius in your new Nissan Leaf for zero-emissions supremacy

A Day in the Life of a Conservative	A Day in the Life of a Liberal
★ 2:00 p.m.	
Walk around the office, remind everyone who the "job creator" is	Walk around the office, try to get coworkers to sign petition to change this year's office Christmas party to a nondenominational winter solstice celebration
★ 3:00 p.m.	
Gas up Hummer, reposition Confederate flag on window, clean homeless person off grille	Pump air in bicycle tires, lecture passing drivers about evils of internal combustion engine
★ 4:00 p.m.	
Stop by drugstore for Vicodin prescription, report suspicious-looking cashier to INS for deportation	Stop by holistic healing center to see if the South American pygmy healing root has arrived in hopes of curing venereal diseases picked up at Burning Man

A Day in the Life of a Conservative	A Day in the Life of a Liberal
★ 5:00 p.m.	
Stop by Walmart, buy booze and ammo	Stop by Whole Foods, spend $60 for a free-range beet salad and a mineral water from France
★ 6:00 p.m.	
Join the guys at Hooters to watch ESPN and ogle the waitstaff over a couple of pitchers	Join fellow tree huggers to block commuter traffic until the city agrees to build a "toad tunnel" allowing frogs to safely cross busy street
★ 7:00 p.m.	
Sit down to family dinner and enjoy a delicious Godfather's pizza in honor of future president Herman Cain	Occupy your local country club, eat the rich, then recycle their monocles and top hats in a wealthy compost heap
★ 8:00 p.m.	
Watch *The O'Reilly Factor* for fair and balanced news	Watch *The Daily Show* for fair and balanced news

A Day in the Life of a Conservative	A Day in the Life of a Liberal
★ *8:30 p.m.*	
Put the kids to bed after reading them *Help Mom! There Are Liberals Under My Bed!*	Put the kids to bed after reading them *Mommy, Mama, and Me*
★ *9:00 p.m.*	
Log on to Hot Air to read new and inventive ways to continue to blame Obama	Log on to Media Matters to read new and inventive ways to continue to blame Bush
★ *10:00 p.m.*	
Have missionary sex with spouse (if on a business trip, have illicit tryst in hotel bathroom with intern)	Invite the neighbors over for Tantric group orgy while listening to Tuvan throat singing
★ *11:00 p.m.*	
Recite prayers, await the Rapture	Smoke joint, fall asleep

"The Democrats are the party of government activism, the party that says government can make you richer, smarter, taller, and get the chickweed out of your lawn. Republicans are the party that says government doesn't work, and then get elected and prove it."

—P. J. O'Rourke

Battle of the Bumper Stickers

There's no better illustration of the stark partisan split than the ideological battle that conservatives and liberals are waging every day on America's roadways.

POPULAR CONSERVATIVE BUMPER STICKERS

★ Don't Blame Me! I Voted For The American

★ Occupy A Job!

★ Does This Ass Make My Car Look Fat? (with a picture of Obama)

★ Global Warming: The #1 Threat To Unicorns

★ I'd Rather Be A Conservative Nut Job Than A Liberal With No Nuts And No Job!

- ★ Environmentalism: Just Another Religious Doomsday Cult
- ★ Work Harder! Millions On Welfare Depend On You!
- ★ I Only Burn Fuel Because Burning Hippies Is Illegal
- ★ Somewhere In Kenya, A Village Is Missing Its Idiot
- ★ Silly Liberal, Paychecks Are For Workers
- ★ If Ignorance Is Bliss, You Must Be One Happy Liberal
- ★ I'd Vote For A Democrat, But I'm Allergic To Nuts
- ★ Stop Global Whining
- ★ Spread My Work Ethic, Not My Wealth
- ★ You Can't Fix Stupid, But You Can Vote It Out

POPULAR LIBERAL BUMPER STICKERS

- ★ Tea Parties Are For Little Girls With Imaginary Friends
- ★ I Refuse To Believe Corporations Are People Until Texas Executes One
- ★ The Republican Party: Our Bridge To The 11th Century

- ★ My President Killed Osama Bin Laden. How About Yours?
- ★ Evolution Is Just A Theory…Kind Of Like Gravity
- ★ Don't Like Socialism? Get Off The Highway
- ★ Insurance Companies Are Republican Death Panels
- ★ May The Fetus You Save Be Gay
- ★ GOP Family Values—Your Rights Begin At Conception And End At Birth
- ★ That Stuff Trickling Down On You Isn't Money
- ★ Killing For Peace Is Like Screwing For Virginity
- ★ Honk If My Taxes Support Your Whiny Teabagging Ass
- ★ Democrats: Cleaning Up Republican Messes Since 1933
- ★ Voting Is Like Driving A Car. Choose (R) To Move Backward. Choose (D) To Move Forward.
- ★ Fox News: Rich People Paying Rich People To Tell Middle Class People To Blame Poor People

"Conservative, n: a statesman who is enamored of existing evils, as distinguished from the Liberal, who wishes to replace them with others."

—Ambrose Bierce

What Conservatives Say vs. What Liberals Hear

Most liberals and conservatives who have spent any time in the partisan trenches quickly discover that even basic attempts at communication can be utterly futile. Thanks to ingrained stereotypes, built-in defense mechanisms, and intense partisan conditioning, a conservative may say one thing, but a liberal is almost certain to hear something else. As you can see here, it's not pretty:

What conservatives say: Obama is a Muslim Kenyan socialist Nazi and probably the Antichrist.
What liberals hear: I was homeschooled by Fox News.

What conservatives say: If we cut taxes on the rich and cut spending, it will create millions of jobs, reduce the deficit, and make the economy boom.
What liberals hear: Unicorns for everybody!

What conservatives say: Democrats are communist, fascist, Nazi socialists.
What liberals hear: I have no idea what any of those words actually mean, I just have no ideas of my own.

What conservatives say: Obamacare is unconstitutional!
What liberals hear: Three cheers for letting the uninsured die!

What conservatives say: We need to crack down on illegal immigration.
What liberals hear: I'm racist and afraid of brown people. Better grill them on an electrified fence before they knock up my daughter.

What conservatives say: We need to defend the institution of marriage and stop the gay agenda.
What liberals hear: I'm a closeted homosexual who likes to frequent airport men's rooms.

What conservatives say: Democrats are coming after your money, your guns, and your God.
What liberals hear: Hey, here's some irrational fear to trick really stupid people into feeling good about voting against their own interests.

What conservatives say: Democrats want to bring your grandmother before a death panel.
What liberals hear: I'm watching Glenn Beck TV and I'm off my meds.

What conservatives say: We need to dismantle the job-killing EPA.

What liberals hear: Hey kids, free arsenic and mercury for everyone!

What conservatives say: We need to reduce our dependency on foreign oil by pursuing oil exploration at home.

What liberals hear: I hate national parks and coastlines! Let's improve them by adding giant oil rigs and pollution. Besides how cute are pelicans when they're covered in oil?

What conservatives say: This is a Christian nation, and our laws should reflect that.

What liberals hear: I'm sick of Jewish people taking more holidays than me.

What conservatives say: Liberals are all a bunch of Hollywood-loving, gun-grabbing, stem-cell-sucking, abortion-promoting, tax-hiking, troop-slandering, gay-marrying socialists who are hell-bent on destroying America.

What liberals hear: Good evening, and welcome to *The Sean Hannity Show.*

What Liberals Say vs. What Conservatives Hear

There's no better luck on the flip side:

What liberals say: We must raise taxes on the top 1% and spread the wealth around.

What conservatives hear: I'm not going to work. Give me money. Take care of my lazy ass.

What liberals say: We must occupy Wall Street and bring down those greedy bastards.

What conservatives hear: I don't shower.

What liberals say: Corporations are NOT people!

What conservatives hear: I hate free markets and would rather live in China!

What liberals say: I'm tired of listening to religious nut cases and puritanical prudes trying to dictate what I do in the bedroom or what I can do with my body.

What conservatives hear: Let's go have sex with a horse and then worship Satan.

What liberals say: The media does not have a liberal bias.

What conservatives hear: Baaaaaaaa. I'm a sheep.

What liberals say: Make love, not war.
What conservatives hear: I heart terrorists!

What liberals say: Republicans hate all poor people, minorities, and the elderly.
What conservatives hear: Hey, it's Kanye West!

What liberals say: Bush wrecked the economy. Everything is Bush's fault!
What conservatives hear: Our plan to fix the economy crapped out so all we got left is "blame the last guy."

What liberals say: Conservatives are all a bunch of uneducated, health-care-denying, waterboard-loving, doomsday-preaching, corporate-crime-forgiving, NRA-worshipping, knuckle-dragging, Bible-banging bigots who have done more to destroy American democracy than Al Qaeda ever dreamed.
What conservatives hear: I hate America, I hate freedom, I hate puppies, and welcome to the *Rachel Maddow Show*.

"What side shall prevail in this epic electoral tilt? Who shall control the future of Fortress America? Will we be, as the Republicans desire, a nation of wealthy, heavily-armed white men, befouling the air and water in a ceaseless quest for profits, beholden to no laws but those of our Lord and Savior Jesus Christ? Or shall we instead embrace the Democrats' vision of a namby-pamby, quasi-socialist republic with an all-homosexual army flamboyantly defending a citizenry suckling at the foul teat of government welfare? The choice is yours, fair maiden America, for the name of this feudal system is Democracy."

—Stephen Colbert

Common Enemies We Can All Agree to Hate

OK, now that it's abundantly clear how hopelessly estranged and deranged the two warring sides have become, it's time to find that elusive common ground.

It's been said that what divides us as a country is not nearly as strong as what unites us. And what could unite us more than our common enemies? With that in mind, let us embark on the path to bipartisan unity by taking a moment to jointly revile some of the most odious miscreants and evildoers that liberals and conservatives can agree to hate.

You can, of course, never go wrong bashing the likes of Al Qaeda, Mahmoud Ahmadinejad, corporate criminals, pedophiles, and people who talk on their cell phones during movies. But if you really want to bond with liberals, try trash-talking the following enemies of freedom, all of whom pose a more immediate threat to our collective sanity.

THE MEDIA

It's a sad commentary on the state of the news media when Americans identify comedian Jon Stewart as the most trusted newsman on television. Whether you think the mainstream media is guilty of liberal or conservative bias, it can usually be counted on to botch the facts and distort the truth in the race to get the story wrong first. Sure, there are some intrepid journalists doing important work, but then there's Piers Morgan. As a whole, the establishment media is a brainless, sensationalistic, and unstoppable force that you can rely on to saturate the airwaves with wall-to-wall coverage of the latest missing blonde girl, ignore the current genocidal war in

Africa, blindly regurgitate partisan talking points, and, occasionally, make up stories out of whole cloth. The best you can hope for these days are partially correct weather and traffic reports.

> *"The press can hold its magnifying glass up to our problems and illuminate problems heretofore unseen, or it can use its magnifying glass to light ants on fire, and then perhaps host a week of shows on the sudden, unexpected dangerous-flaming-ant epidemic. If we amplify everything, we hear nothing."*
>
> —Jon Stewart at the Rally to Restore Sanity and/or Fear

TSA AGENTS

It's not their fault that their job sucks, it's the evil pleasure they derive from patting down an eighty-seven-year old grandma who might be concealing a four-ounce tube of hemorrhoid medicine in her denture case. Or, in one actual case, going through a woman's luggage, finding a sex toy, and leaving a handwritten note that said, "GET YOUR FREAK ON GIRL." The TSA's motto is

"Your safety is our priority," but a popular Internet meme suggested some fitting alternatives: "We are now free to move about your pants," "We handle more packages than USPS," "It's not a grope. It's a freedom pat," and "If we did our job any better we'd have to buy you dinner first."

PORK-BARREL SPENDERS

You and your liberal pals should be able to agree that the following actual uses of taxpayer money (approved by Democrats and Republicans alike) should be considered criminal: $143 million to protect the Giant Lava Lamp in Soap Lake, Washington, against terrorist attack; $10 million to protect a toilet seat art museum in Alamo Heights, Texas, against terrorist attack; $7 million spent by the Army each year to sponsor NASCAR Sprint Cup driver Ryan Newman; nearly $600,000 to study why chimps throw feces; over $175,000 to study how cocaine enhances the sex drive of Japanese quail; over $6,000 to purchase snow cone ice-making machines for emergencies in Michigan; and $800,000 in "stimulus funds" spent to study the impact of a "genital-washing program" on men in South Africa. This is particularly wasteful because surely there are men in America who would gladly wash their genitals for half that amount.

OFFSHORERS

When it comes to big business and tax policy, Republicans and Democrats agree on virtually nothing. But one area where both sides should be able to find common ground is in vilifying those soulless bastards who exploit huge corporate tax breaks, only to move all the jobs offshore. How about we pass a constitutional amendment so the next time they need a bailout, they automatically get re-routed to a call center in India where a guy named "Bob" will happily waste three hours of their time before arbitrarily disconnecting them.

WESTBORO BAPTIST CHURCH

Another hate group masquerading as a church, this loathsome assemblage of mouth-breathing Neanderthals has made a name for itself by desecrating the American flag and picketing the funerals of soldiers and famous people with their gay-bashing placards. Even the KKK got involved in protesting these jackasses. Yes, this is something even you and your local Grand Dragon or Imperial Wizard can agree on. The Westboro Baptist Church freaks are such heartless and vile souls that no right-thinking Republican, Democrat, or reputable institution could ever possibly defend them—with the notable exception of the U.S. Supreme Court, which upheld their right to terrorize people at funerals. Stupid First Amendment.

OWNERS AND PLAYERS WHO GIVE US STRIKES AND LOCKOUTS

One place Republicans, Democrats, and independents should be able to find common ground is in their hatred of greedy billionaires and spoiled millionaires who take away our sports when they can't work out their differences. Players, you are grown men who get paid obscene amounts of money to play with a ball. Owners, you are already billionaires, not to mention all the chicks you get just for saying, "By the way, I own the Dallas Mavericks." No one feels sorry for either of you, so figure it out. It is with one clear voice we say, "Suck it up, professional sports." No American wins when Lakers vs. Celtics is replaced by *A Very Kardashian Christmas*.

REALITY SHOW STARS

Is there any bigger waste of time than reality television? OK, maybe listening to people talk about reality television. With all the problems in this country, why do we have to hear about these people every day? Who cares which washed up celebrity is a better dancer? Did we really need to see Tom DeLay's gyrating ass on television (an image so horrifying, no amount of bleach could remove it from our eyes)? Do those "real housewives" look like anyone you've ever met in real life? You're having a fight in a kitchen about some soup—for the love of God, why? And seriously, enough shows about freakishly large families. Isn't flying terrifying enough without the prospect of getting stuck on a twelve-hour flight behind *Kate Plus Eight*? Please bring back the one reality show we could all agree on: *COPS!*

"I view America like this: 70 to 80 percent [are] pretty reasonable people that truthfully, if they sat down, even on contentious issues, would get along. And the other 20 percent of the country run it."

—Jon Stewart

CHAPTER 4

Basic Training

"Irreverence is the champion of liberty and its only sure defense."

—Mark Twain

There's a right way to engage liberals in combat and a wrong way. The right way will enable you to make forceful arguments, win hearts and minds, and be greeted as a liberator. The wrong way will alienate your opponents, make them harden their position, and get you kicked out of public places.

Unfortunately, due to inadequate preparation and training—or sheer self-delusion—many people embark on the wrong path. To help you gird for battle and avert certain disaster, we'll show you in this chapter how to avoid key pitfalls, pick the right fights, hone your bullshit detector, and turn arguments to your advantage by following some basic rules of engagement.

 "The definition of insanity is doing the same thing over and over again and expecting different results."

—Albert Einstein, attributed

The Seven Habits of Highly Ineffective Partisans

As with many things in life, we are often our own worst enemies. These seven habits are like kryptonite to the partisan warrior and must be painstakingly avoided.

1. PEDDLING CONSPIRACY THEORIES

Tempting as it may be to try and convince a liberal that Obama is a secret Muslim sleeper agent who was born in Kenya or that FEMA is plotting to open concentration camps to intern U.S. citizens, there's no faster way to undermine your own cause than trafficking in conspiracy theories. Even if you feel you have rock-solid intelligence from the Nigerian prince who emailed you directly, don't go there. You just end up looking like an idiot. There are plenty of good arguments to make without bringing in the vast conspiracy of little green men on the grassy knoll. And besides, as anyone who has worked in government will tell you, the government isn't competent enough to pull off a decent conspiracy.

2. USING NAZI ANALOGIES

George W. Bush wasn't Hitler. Obama isn't Hitler. The next Republican president liberals will be tempted to call Hitler won't be Hitler either. Hitler was Hitler. Enough already, because do you know who else liked over-the-top political analogies? Hitler.

3. LETTING LIBERALS MAKE YOU CRAZY

Liberals will undoubtedly drive you nutty with their brick-like imperviousness to reality and common sense. But remember, that's their goal. They want to see the veins pop out of your forehead and cartoon steam emit from your ears. Don't let them succeed. No matter what they say, keep a cool head. If you end up having a Charlie Sheen-style meltdown and find yourself blurting out that you have "tiger blood" and "fire-breathing fists," while insisting, "I'm not bipolar, I'm bi-winning, I win here and I win there," you're definitely not winning.

4. FAILING TO SUPPORT
YOUR ARGUMENTS WITH FACTS

Making an argument without supporting facts is the difference between talking and simply moving air. Sure you can argue, for example, that Obama is the worst president ever, but it's better to support it by stating he has the worst job record of any U.S. president since World War II. Sure you can say Obama is driving us into financial ruin, but it's better to remind your opponent he presided over the first downgrade of the U.S. credit rating in history. You wouldn't go into a gun fight without ammunition, and facts are your Teflon-coated bullets.

5. RESORTING TO NAME-CALLING AT THE OUTSET

It's generally not good strategy to begin an argument by calling your opponent a godless, America-hating socialist or a spineless, tofu-licking moron. Ad hominem attacks are a sign of weakness—a tactic that ineffective partisans resort to when they're too lazy or ill-informed to make real arguments. Instead, save your insults for detonation after you've *lost* an argument, when all else has failed (see After-*words*: 125,000 Ways to Insult Liberals). For example, if you've just tried to argue that Obama is coddling terrorists and your opponent points out that he has orchestrated the killings of more top terrorists than any Nobel Peace Prize winner in history, that's a good time to hit the eject button and deploy your parachute as you say, "At least I'm not an unemployed, bongo-playing, hippie weasel like you."

6. MAKING SWEEPING GENERALIZATIONS

Even if you believe it's true that *all* liberals hate America, freedom, capitalism, the military, God, and kittens, the problem with making those kinds of flat declarations is that you create too much territory to defend. It also makes it much easier for your opponent to knock down your arguments. Always be specific, and only state what is necessary to make your case. Argue instead, for example, that *all MSNBC hosts* hate America, freedom, the military, capitalism, God, and kittens.

7. ARGUING WITH IDIOTS

"Do not argue with an idiot," Mark Twain once said. "He will drag you down to his level and beat you with experience." Better to save the oxygen for those capable of rational discourse. If you must argue with an idiot, different rules apply. Take humorist Dave Barry's advice: (1) drink liquor; (2) make things up; (3) use meaningless but weighty-sounding words and phrases ("vis-à-vis," "per se," "ipso facto," "ergo"); (4) use snappy and irrelevant comebacks ("You're begging the question," "You're being defensive," "You're so linear"); and (5) go ahead and compare your opponent to Hitler.

"I argue very well. Ask any of my remaining friends. I can win an argument on any topic, against any opponent. People know this and steer clear of me at parties. Often as a sign of their great respect, they don't even invite me."

—Dave Barry

Do You Suffer from Argumentile Dysfunction?

Now let's identify whether you're predisposed to any of the seven deadly habits. Answer these questions about how you would handle yourself in the following situations.

1. You're standing around the water cooler listening to a colleague rant about why the rich need a big tax hike. She's arguing that the top 1% own the majority of the wealth but don't carry their fair share of the tax burden. Which of the following would you do?

_____A. Quickly excuse yourself, saying you seem to have accidentally wound up in communist China.

_____B. Explain that the poor could get rich, too, if they ever tried working. And no, drum circle leader doesn't count because it isn't a paying job.

_____C. Remind her that raising taxes is exactly what Hitler did before he attempted to create a master race of liberal democratic socialists.

_____D. Tell her she's not carrying her fair share of the workload around the office, but you're not going around telling everyone she needs a pay cut.

_____E. Argue that giving money back to the people who pay the highest taxes will help to spur investment and create jobs that benefit the economy as a whole.

2. You're showing off your gun collection to your new neighbor, and you discover that he's a staunch gun-control advocate. He says that guns endanger everyone's lives. Which of the following would you do?

_____A. "Accidentally" blow off his foot.

_____B. Explain that if guns kill people, pencils

        misspell words, matches cause arson, cars make people drive drunk, and spoons make Rosie O'Donnell fat.

_____C. Pull out a copy of the Second Amendment and ask him to read it out loud and identify which words he doesn't understand.

_____D. Ask him what he plans to use to fend off would-be attackers, his ACLU card or his lawyer?

_____E. Explain that you've had extensive training in gun safety and offer to take him hunting.

3. A friend confesses after Bible study that she's thinking of voting for a Democrat in the next election. Which of the following would you do?

_____A. Wish her well on her journey to the fiery pits of everlasting hell.

_____B. Explain that a vote for Obama is a vote for the Antichrist.

_____C. Tell her Jesus would never vote for a Democrat because he was a supply-sider who thought a progressive tax structure unfairly punished the wealthy.

_____D. Tell her it's a shame because when the Rapture comes, she'll be left behind to be ravaged by earthquakes and eaten by zombies.

_____E.   Challenge her with tough questions and demonstrate how voting that way is not in her self-interest.

If you answered E to all of the previous questions, you're ready to move on to the next section. If not, this may help explain why you haven't been winning many arguments lately (and possibly why you don't get invited to social functions anymore).

"A diplomat...is a person who can tell you to go to hell in such a way that you actually look forward to the trip."

—Caskie Stinnett

How Not to Be an Asshole

Tempted as you may be to blurt out obscenities, hurl insults, or pepper-spray your opponent, successful arguing strategy (and the laws of polite society) require that you employ more civilized tactics.

The following chart will show you how to channel your fury in a way that—while admittedly less satisfying than, say, telling your opponent to go perform an anatomically impossible sex act—will help encourage better diplomatic relations.

What You'll Be Tempted to Say	How to Translate that into Diplo-Speak
"Are you completely freaking insane?"	"I'm not sure I'm following the reasoning behind your argument."
"Did your lobotomy leave a scar?"	"Do you honestly believe that?"
"Which dark crevice of your ass did you pull that from?"	"How do you back up that claim?"
"Stupid hippie weasel."	"I can't identify with what you're saying."
"What do the demons say when they come for you at night?"	"How did you arrive at that conclusion?"

What You'll Be Tempted to Say	How to Translate that into Diplo-Speak
"Does your cable company only carry the Fox Network?"	"Let me suggest some news sources that report actual facts."
"Do I need to speak slower, with fewer syllables?"	"I'm not sure we're communicating."
"I've never met a bigger phony in my life."	"Nice to meet you, Mrs. Pelosi."
"Isn't it great that we live in a country where even a total douche bag like yourself is free to utter whatever mindless drivel pops into his head?"	"You have a right to your opinion."

What You'll Be Tempted to Say	How to Translate that into Diplo-Speak
"Did you learn to be an America-hating terrorist sympathizer at your liberal arts college, or did you pick it up while interning for the Taliban?"	"Where did you get your unconventional ideas?"
"If I had $100 for every time you said something true, I'd be poor as shit."	"Better recheck your facts, Senator Reid."
"Your parents were clearly brother and sister."	"You obviously come from a very close family."
"Did you eat a lot of paint chips when you were a kid?"	"You must have had a very challenging childhood."

What You'll Be Tempted to Say	How to Translate that into Diplo-Speak
"You're spewing more bullshit than a rodeo."	"Do you have even one fact to back that up?"
"How is it even possible for a sentient being to arrive at that kind of breathtakingly idiotic conclusion?"	"If I agreed with you, we'd both be wrong."
"Tell me, you godless, gun-grabbing socialist, do you Tweet your insanity too?"	"You may want to reconsider your use of social media."
"What planet do you fucking live on?"	"I think we have radically different notions of what constitutes reality."

"If you've got them by the balls, their hearts and minds will follow."

—Anonymous

The Ten Commandments of Partisan Warfare

Here is your guide to becoming a model partisan.

1. USE HUMOR AS A WEAPON

Making humorous observations—and demonstrating an ability to laugh at yourself—can be an effective tool to help disarm your opponents. They'll be much more likely to listen to the next thing you have to say. Once you've cracked a joke or two and lulled them into a sense of complacency, that's when you move in for the kill. If funny isn't your thing, quote professional quipsters like Dennis Miller or unintentional comedians like Joe Biden, and bear in mind what Will Rogers once said: "There's no trick to being a humorist when you have the whole government working for you."

Example: "I looked up 'politics' in the dictionary, and it's actually a combination of two words: 'poli', which means many, and 'tics', which means 'bloodsuckers.'"
—*Jay Leno*

2. KEEP IT SIMPLE

Making long-winded arguments to liberals will get you nowhere because their attention will likely start to wander off as they daydream about all the taxes that have yet to be raised, businesses that have yet to be over-regulated, and why gay Marxist Muslim illegal immigrants have not yet been granted the right to open drive-thru abortion clinics in churches. That's why you need to have some pithy sound bites at your disposal to use as openers or rejoinders. We're not suggesting that you dumb down your arguments. But you should try to distill your basic message to a slogan you could fit on a cardboard sign. (If it doesn't work, then you'll have a handy piece of cardboard you can use to beat them over the head.)

Example: "Government's view of the economy could be summed up in a few short phrases: If it moves, tax it. If it keeps moving, regulate it. And if it stops moving, subsidize it." —*Ronald Reagan*

3. FRAME THE DEBATE TO YOUR ADVANTAGE

Always stay on the offensive and make your case by presenting each issue according to your beliefs and values, *not theirs*. If you let your adversary define the terms and frame the discussion, they win.

Example: Here's how you might frame an argument to a pro-choice liberal, courtesy of P. J. O'Rourke: "No one is fond of taking responsibility for his actions, but consider how much you'd have to hate free will to come up with a political platform that advocates killing unborn babies but not convicted murderers. A callous pragmatist might favor abortion and capital punishment. A devout Christian would sanction neither. But it takes years of therapy to arrive at the liberal point of view."

4. RIDICULE THE OPPOSITION

As the famed left-wing rabble-rouser Saul Alinsky advises in his classic tome *Rules for Radicals* (which some Tea Partiers have recently adapted for their own tactical purposes), "Ridicule is man's most potent weapon. It's hard to counterattack ridicule, and it infuriates the opposition, which then reacts to your advantage." This may explain why left-wingers are always so infuriated—they're so easy to ridicule!

Examples: "President Obama will begin a three-state bus tour. I believe the three states are confusion, delusion, and desperation." —*Jay Leno.* "You can always tell when Obama's negotiations with the Republicans are winding down, because he's missing his watch and his lunch money." —*Bill Maher*. "Many people are complaining that Obama is becoming too scripted. Last night, he was having an intimate moment with Michelle, and she said, 'Wait, are you reading the Teleprompter?'" —*Jimmy Fallon*

5. HIGHLIGHT HYPOCRISY

Nothing undermines an argument faster than exposing hypocritical behavior, contradictory statements, and wholesale fakery—either on the part of your opponents or on the part of the politicians they're defending. There are few sights as satisfying as watching exposed hypocrites grasp at fig leaves to cover their shame.

Examples: Hollywood liberals lecturing about energy conservation before ducking into stretch limos or flying off in their private jets; Michelle Obama promoting healthy eating as part of her anti-obesity campaign, while being spotted feasting on ribs, cheese-burgers, and chocolate milkshakes; and, as columnist Charles Krauthammer once described the Occupy Wall Street crowd, "Starbucks-sipping, Levi's-clad, iPhone-clutching protesters [who] denounce corporate America, even as they weep for Steve Jobs, corporate titan, billionaire eight times over."

6. DAZZLE THEM WITH METAPHORS

You can pack your arguments with extra punch through strategic use of metaphors and analogies. Not only will they help to illustrate your points more vividly, but if you can employ a little humor, you might even coax a chuckle out of your opponents to help lower their defenses.

Example: When a liberal makes a ridiculous claim, such as saying that all of our problems can be solved by bigger government and more spending, don't just say it's ridiculous. Use an analogy: "Giving money and power to government is like giving whiskey and car keys to teenage boys." —*P.J. O'Rourke*

7. USE LIBERALS' OWN WORDS AGAINST THEM

One of the best ways to make a convincing argument to a liberal is to let another liberal do it for you. Any time you can quote a liberal to support your point, it's a twofer: you cite an authority that is unimpeachable in their minds, and you make their heads hurt as they struggle with the cognitive dissonance.

Example: When they say we should raise taxes, despite the fact that we're in a recession, quote President Obama, who said in 2009, "The last thing you want to do is raise taxes in the middle of a recession because that would just suck up—take more demand out of the economy and put business further in a hole." Or when they argue in favor of raising the debt ceiling, point out that when Obama was a senator back in 2006, he said, "The fact that we are here today to debate raising America's debt limit is a sign of leadership failure. It is a sign that the U.S. government can't pay its own bills." Tell them it's no wonder their president has such a hard time pushing his policies when he doesn't even agree with himself. (You can find more damning quotes from liberals in Chapter 8.)

8. MAKE YOUR OPPONENTS DEFEAT THEMSELVES

One of the most effective arguing techniques, utilized by lawyers and others skilled in the art of persuasion, simply involves posing a series of leading questions. It's known as the Socratic method, and it's easy to employ. All you need to do is ask questions that will box in your opponents and expose the gaping holes in their thinking. Demonstrating that someone is wrong is always more effective than telling someone they're wrong.

Example: When a liberal argues that the rich need to start paying their fair share of taxes, try a line of questioning like this: "Do you think it's fair that the top 1 percent of earners pay about 40 percent of all income taxes, or that the top 10 percent pay around 70 percent? Don't you think they're already paying enough? And what about the 47 percent of Americans who don't pay any federal income taxes? Shouldn't we be asking them to chip in their fair share, rather than punishing those who are already shouldering most of the tax burden?"

9. EXPLOIT LIBERAL WISHY-WASHINESS

One of the great things about arguing with liberals is they spend so much time arguing with themselves that they do a lot of the work for you. It's their Achilles heel, and you can exploit it by showing liberals the various ways in which their leaders are failing to fight for their values, or—when faced with Republican opposition— cave in like a wet sand castle at high tide.

Example: Many liberals remain lukewarm about supporting President Obama, disappointed that he hasn't turned water into wine and cured cancer like they thought he would. When they talk about their disillusionment, "they sound like somebody who took an Ambien and woke up naked outside," quipped Dennis Miller. Remind them that Obama voted to extend the Bush tax cuts, kept Gitmo open, doubled down in Afghanistan, and has done nothing on climate change. Your goal is to sap their enthusiasm and make them question whether it's even worth voting for someone who doesn't stand up for what he believes in. That's as good as winning an argument.

10. LAUNCH A SNEAK ATTACK

If liberals think they are talking to a hopeless conservative, you may never get a chance to win them over because they'll shun you as they would Rush Limbaugh at a NOW convention. That's why in some instances, it can be strategically useful to pretend to be a moderate or a conservative who is open to persuasion. The goal is to rope them in, thinking they may be able to convert you, and then unleash a Trojan horse-style sneak attack when they're least expecting it.

Example: Start by bad-mouthing a conservative (say, Sarah Palin or Pat Robertson) to build street cred. Take it up a notch by grumbling about how Wall Street is plotting to destroy America. Mention you've decided to vote against the Republican candidate in the next election. Suddenly you will find yourself welcomed into the liberal inner sanctum, invited to Hollywood award ceremonies, offered discounts on abortions, and given Kool-Aid (don't drink it!). There are lots of things you can do once you're on the inside: become a mole or parcel out extremely bad advice. Or if all goes well, you can angle your way into becoming a featured speaker at an Occupy protest. Once the cameras are rolling, use the opportunity to denounce the idiocy of Occupiers from the podium—quickly, before naked hippies wrestle you to the ground. Get the footage on YouTube immediately. Gripe loudly about the intolerance of Occupiers while making the rounds on the talk show circuit, and then secure a book deal. Battle won.

> *"I understand my critics are fixated and pathologically disoriented, but they are my opponents. Why would I try to correct them?"*
>
> **—Newt Gingrich**

How to Avoid Unhinged Lunatics

There's nothing wrong with occasionally mixing it up with liberals who have extreme views. It's the ones who have extreme personality disorders that you should be concerned about. You know, those totally incapable of having an intelligent, thoughtful discussion about anything. They bicker instead of argue, rant instead of talk, and parrot instead of think.

These kinds of sociopaths can be found anywhere—

ambushing perfect strangers at cocktail parties, holding entire families hostage at holiday time, and scarring their Facebook pages with Unabomber-level diatribes.

There is no use wasting perfectly good oxygen arguing with these people. You'll be much better off—and cut down on your Xanax bills—if you focus your energies on reasonable people capable of passing a field sanity test. Here's how to administer it:

★ Do they become instantly irate at the slightest of triggers? For example, if you just say the words "Palin" or "Bachmann," do their faces turn visibly red and do their neck veins begin pulsating?

★ In place of the usual expletives, do they use "Fox," "Bush," "Scalia," "Boehner," "Santorum," or "teabagger"?

★ When you mention domestic terrorists, do they correct you and insist they be called "Al Qaeda Americans"?

★ Did they drive up in a car that has more bumper stickers than actual paint? Follow-up bonus: Do the majority of those stickers include quotes from Gandhi, visualizing world peace, or hugging kids with nuclear arms?

★ Do they believe in a trilateral conspiracy that

involves the Heritage Foundation, British Petroleum, and Mr. Burns from *The Simpsons*?

★ At any point in the conversation, do they try and get you to join a union, class action lawsuit, or an animal rights group for marsupials?

★ Have they been "occupying" the restroom stall for more than an hour?

★ Do they show signs of cognitive impairment? For example, can they be seen attending an anti-Wall Street rally and hoisting a sign that says "U.S. out of my uterus!" without even realizing they're in the wrong place?

★ When they talk about regulating people or corporations, do they become sexually aroused?

★ Do they display a pathological fear of opposing viewpoints? For example, do they proudly restrict their intake of news and information to what they read on left-wing blogs, the message board at their local food co-op, or the pamphlets they were handed at the last Green Anti-globalization S&M Festival?

★ Do their kids ask mall Santas for more entitlement spending?

★ Do they travel in large groups just in case they need a human microphone?

★ Do they begin sweating profusely at the mere mention of fiscal responsibility?

★ Did they star in *Good Will Hunting*?

★ Have they already staked a Winfrey/Baldwin 2016 sign into their lawn?

If the liberal in question exhibits any of these behavior patterns, he or she has failed the field sanity test. Do yourself a favor—back away slowly and avoid these people as you would Charlie Sheen at a cocaine and hooker convention. Nothing good will ever come of talking to them.

Anyone else is fair game.

 "The enemy isn't liberalism. The enemy isn't conservatism. The enemy is bullshit."

—Lars-Erik Nelson

How to Detect Bullshit

Let's state the obvious. Liberals love to bullshit. We're not just talking about the professionals in Washington. Your average liberal on the street is skilled at slinging it too.

To combat bullshit, it's important to first define what it is and what makes it so insidious.

"Bullshit is a greater enemy of the truth than lies are," says Harry Frankfurt, who literally wrote the book *On Bullshit*. Bullshitters, Frankfurt says, are distinguished by the fact that they couldn't care less about whether what they are saying is true. They have a completely different agenda. Bullshitters are mainly concerned with trying to wow, distract, or manipulate their audience, and they'll simply cherry-pick facts or make up things to fit their needs.

That's why bullshitters are such menaces to society. Their total lack of regard for the truth gives them free rein to manipulate people willy-nilly, so long as no one calls them on it. They also have one thing in common: they're trying to conceal something.

To help you calibrate your bullshit detector, here's a guide to the various bullshitting life forms that you are likely to encounter and what they are trying to hide.

THE FACT FABRICATORS

What they do: They present you with the "straight facts," which are actually faux facts that they likely found on some lefty blog or read on leaflets they picked up at a green festival, thinking they were marijuana rolling papers. They'll make up anything to support their crumbling arguments, mismatch disjointed pieces of information to form a fact-esque facade, and reject any inconvenient facts as biased and likely fascist. When cornered by incontrovertible facts (e.g., gravity or the latest employment figures), they'll simply throw up a smoke screen and declare the facts to be open to debate.

What they're hiding: That they no longer know the difference between fact and fiction, and worse, they don't care.

THE KNOWLEDGE SUPREMACISTS

What they do: They attempt to dazzle their audiences with their sheer volume of knowledge on any given topic, most of it pulled directly from their asses. They spew it faster than you can Google it. Their goal with this information assault is to beat you into submission and assert their superior opinions. They base everything on information sources that you could not possibly have access to, which is sort of the equivalent of saying, "I have a girlfriend, but she lives in Canada."

What they're hiding: The fact that they're suffering from the intellectual equivalent of "penis envy."

THE CREDENTIAL FALSIFIERS

What they do: They claim to have unique life experiences or qualifications that you don't, which therefore validate their views and negate yours. For example, they may refer to their military training and combat experience when it turns out that all they ever did was play *World of Warcraft*.

What they're hiding: The fact that they're average and ill-informed.

THE "TRUTHINESS" TELLERS

What they do: They cling to the truths that come straight from their gut, rather than from reality. As defined by comedian Stephen Colbert, "truthiness" refers to an individual's preference for believing in what he or she wishes to be true rather than what is known to be true.

What they're hiding: Their utter terror of reality.

THE BULLSHIT ACOLYTES

What they do: They perpetuate left-wing spin through empty sloganeering and mindless repetition of Democratic talking points crafted by the likes of Nancy Pelosi, Michael Moore, and George Soros.

What they're hiding: That sheep vote Democrat.

How to Trip Up a Bullshitter

Good bullshitters can be hard to spot, but you may be able to trip them up by their failure to answer basic questions or inability to support their claims. Next time you smell the stink, take the following steps:

1. Hit them with simple questions they probably won't be expecting, such as "How do you know that?"; "How can you prove that?"; or if it's something completely obvious: "So what you're saying is, NBC News, *The New York Times*, NPR, and every other news agency in the world is wrong, and you, an unemployed, alcoholic Xbox player, are right?"

2. If you suspect they're just blindly spewing rhetoric or unthinkingly parroting left-wing spin, challenge them to provide specifics. For example, make them explain exactly how Wall Street hedge fund managers are plotting to destroy America, how health-care reform will lower anyone's health-care costs, or specifically how Democrats think they can tax our way to prosperity.

3. As they grasp to substantiate their claims, watch for telltale signs of lying, such as lack of eye

contact, a scratch to the nose, or words coming out of their mouths forming sentences. Consider responses such as "I read it in a Daily Kos discussion thread," "I heard it at an Occupy Berkeley spirit cleanse," or "I saw it in a peyote vision" to be admissions that they see the world through bullshit-colored glasses.

4. Call them on their deceit, show them where they went wrong, and suggest that they leave the bullshitting to trained professionals, like Barack Obama spouting off poetic nonsense from his Teleprompter, Nancy Pelosi harping about evil Republicans while struggling to move her face, or Joe Biden trying to speak through the duct tape Obama has strapped over his mouth.

How to Spot Logical Fallacies

If you've ever been part of an argument that feels disingenuous, grossly oversimplified, rigged against you, or which makes no earthly sense, then you've probably encountered a logical fallacy. They're the one-legged stools of faulty reasoning that liberals rely on to prop up many of their ridiculous ideas.

Some liberals intentionally use logical fallacies to play manipulative mind games, while others may inadvertently stick a finger in the eye of reason. Whatever the case, learning to recognize common logical fallacies—and calling your opponent on them—will help you to immediately deflate many bogus lines of attack.

Or, if you're feeling Machiavellian, you can also deliberately use these techniques yourself to try and pull a fast one on an unwitting opponent. In fact, you may spot a few fallacies employed for comedic ends elsewhere in this book.

FALSE CHOICE

Offering only two options for consideration when there are clearly other valid choices.

Example: We can either rely on Washington to fix our broken economic system, or we can rely on the thieves and greed-mongers on Wall Street who got us into this mess in the first place.

STRAW MAN

Oversimplifying, exaggerating, caricaturing, or otherwise misrepresenting your position without regard to fact. In doing this, your opponent sets up a figurative straw man that he can easily knock down to prove his point.

Example: Republicans think no one should have to pay taxes and we should disband the government. And where would that leave us? In a state of anarchy, ruled by roving militias. Is that really the kind of America you want your children to grow up in?

SLIPPERY SLOPE

Leaping to wild, sometimes inexplicable conclusions—going, say, from step one to step two and then all the way to step ten without establishing any discernible connection. By using this kind of leapfrog logic, a person can come to any conclusion he damn well pleases.

Example: If Republicans repeal health-care reform, next they will repeal Social Security, Medicare, civil rights, voting rights, child labor laws, and take us back to the nineteenth century.

AD HOMINEM

Leveling a personal attack in an attempt to discredit an argument rather than addressing the argument itself.

Example: "[Sarah Palin is] a vainglorious braggart, a liar, a whiner, a professional victim…a know-it-all, a chiseler, a bully who sells patriotism like a pimp, and the leader of a strange family of inbred weirdoes straight out of *The Hills Have Eyes*." —*Bill Maher*

HASTY GENERALIZATION

Jumping to a far-reaching conclusion based on scant evidence or forming a stereotype based on a single flimsy example or two.

Example: Conservatives love to moralize about family values, but they're all a bunch of hypocrites who are either banging their mistresses or tapping their toes in the men's room looking for gay hookers. Just look at Newt Gingrich and Larry Craig.

APPEAL TO AUTHORITY

Invoking an authority figure—whether a politician, a famous person, or a so-called expert—to prove an argument rather than substantiating the argument itself.

Example: Of course it's time to raise taxes on the rich. Warren Buffet said so.

APPEAL TO FEAR

Preying on people's fears in an attempt to skirt any need for evidence or analysis about an issue.

Example: If you don't do your part to stop global warming by installing compact fluorescent light bulbs, the ice caps are going to melt and turn your living room into a well-lit aquarium.

THE BANDWAGON APPEAL

Demonstrating that an argument is valid based on the fact that it is popularly accepted or because "everyone is doing it."

Example: A majority of Americans now believe that marijuana should be legal, so how about uncuffing me, officer, and giving back my Chong Bong?

REDUCTIO AD ABSURDUM

Attempting to disprove an opponent's position by taking it to an absurd conclusion.

Example: You support checking immigration documents for anyone suspected of being in the country illegally? Oh, so you think we should be living in a Nazi police state where cops go around to everyone saying, "*Achtung!* Your papers please! *Schnell!*"

FALSE CAUSE

This fallacy, known among logic buffs as *post hoc ergo propter hoc*, is based on the assertion that because one action or event occurs and is followed by another, the first must have caused the second.

Example: When the Texas Rangers played in the World Series, George W. Bush threw out the first pitch two years in a row. The Rangers lost two years in a row. Bush caused the Rangers to lose.

"If you can't beat them, arrange to have them beaten."

—George Carlin

How to Win When You Can't Win Them Over

As a passionate partisan who's determined to convert liberals to your way of thinking, you want what anyone would want: to watch them grovel on their knees as they recant their beliefs and praise you for showing them the path to salvation.

But the reality is that you can do everything right, make flawless arguments, and still find yourself getting nowhere. Some liberals are so unteachably ignorant, so self-righteously closed-minded, there is literally nothing you can say—or no legal torture method you can employ—to enlighten them. If you're planning to mix it up with liberals who fit that profile, you'll need a blunter instrument than this book with which to beat them over the head.

Fortunately, there are a few other important ways in which you can still declare victory when you haven't won them over. You can unfurl your "Mission Accomplished" banner if you succeed in doing any of the following:

1. **Humiliate your opponent.** If you can undercut your opponent's arguments while making him look foolish in the process, you may not win a convert, but you can emancipate yourself—and perhaps a few grateful bystanders—from the spell of their bullshit.

2. **Sew your opponent with seeds of self doubt.** If your opponent gives you everything he's got and then finds himself trapped under the weight of his own inadequacy—making fruitless counterarguments or being reduced to speechlessness—that's a good time to walk away. Let him fester in his own silent insufficiency. One day those seeds may bloom into giant flowers of debilitating self-doubt.

3. **Win over the crowd.** When you're arguing with a liberal in front of other people—at a dinner party, for example—you can score a major victory simply by making superior arguments. Your goal is to

appear more knowledgeable, more reasonable, and more logical, while exposing your opponent as ill-prepared, hypocritical, or simply clueless. Do that, and it doesn't matter whether you win over your adversary because you will have won the crowd.

4. **Win a war of attrition.** You may not be able to bring someone around overnight, but with patience and persistence, and possibly with the help of enough alcohol, you may eventually break your opponents down and get them to admit the folly of their ways—or at least stop voting Democrat.

Chapter 5

How to Win Friends While Antagonizing People

LUKE: Your thoughts betray you, Father. I feel the good in you, the conflict.

DARTH VADER: There is no conflict.

LUKE: You couldn't bring yourself to kill me before, and I don't believe you'll destroy me now.

DARTH VADER: You underestimate the power of the Dark Side. If you will not fight, then you will meet your destiny.

—Star Wars: Return of the Jedi

E veryone says you shouldn't argue politics in polite company. Wrong! Polite company is the best place to hone your combat skills. If you sit around waiting for impolite company to come along, your feeble skills will be no match for their pitchforks or their torches.

You have to start somewhere, so who better to prey on than your friends and loved ones or the guy in the next cubicle whose name you can't remember? Navigating these minefields, however, requires special training. To help you bait and baffle your adversaries (while avoiding interpersonal disaster), this chapter offers some essential "DOs" and "DON'Ts" for dealing with several potentially hazardous combat zones.

How to Survive Family Sparring Matches

For some families it's an annual ritual: Everyone is sitting around the dinner table, enjoying a lovely Thanksgiving meal and getting into the holiday spirit, when Cousin Blowhard says, "And Lord, I'm thankful that Americans are beginning to recognize the disparity in wealth between the 99% and the 1%." Uncle Max takes the bait and says, "I don't think God needs an update on your socialist class warfare." Pretty soon the conversation descends into a back-and-forth volley of pronouncements, such as, "Don't you realize we're celebrating a holiday based on Anglo Imperialism?"; "Did you learn that in your hippie college? Was that covered in socialist studies? You should be learning computers!"; "You have no respect for my vegan dietary preferences!"; and "I can't believe I helped your parents with tuition for this crap. I should have gone to Vegas!" At which point chairs are pushed back and dishes are cleared, while your mother weeps quietly in the corner.

The thing about arguing with family is, you're in it for the long haul; they're as stuck with you as you are with them. That gives you a little more leeway, so everyone knows they can push the envelope further than they would in other situations. For that reason, a few basic rules apply.

★ **DO** crack jokes to disarm your opponents and lull them into a false sense of complacency. Keep an ample supply of alcohol at the ready; nobody bites the hand that gets them drunk. Or, an even better idea, ply them with coffee or Red Bull (people who are wired on caffeine are more susceptible to persuasion, according to an actual scientific study).

★ **DO** attempt to recruit impressionable family

members to your side, particularly when they're young; for example, give your seven-year-old nephew a $100 bill and explain that he should keep it in a safe place, because one day liberals will try to take it away.

★ **DO** consider holding an intervention if you are truly worried about a family member's well-being—for example, if that same nephew later considers attending a liberal arts college in the northeast because it offers courses such as The Sexuality of Terrorism and Marxist Cinema, with guest lecturer Michael Moore, it's time to step in.

★ **DON'T** let the family blowhard hold the dinner table hostage. Fact-check him right then and there using your smart phone or iPad. Counter him point-for-point, fire off contradictory statistics, and inform him he scored a "Pants on Fire" on PolitiFact's Truth-O-Meter test. Remember, liberals hate facts. They get in the way of oversimplifications and bleeding hearts. It's like sunlight to a vampire.

★ **DON'T** proselytize to your children about your politics; they'll just rebel. First they'll start experimenting by reading liberal blogs (also known as "gateway blogs"). Then they'll progress to binge use of Democratic talking points at weekend social gatherings. Before you know it they'll have developed a habitual dependency on liberal dogma, for which there may be no rehabilitation. (See: Schultz, Ed)

★ **DON'T** try to get in the last word with a liberal loved one at his or her own funeral. It comes off as insensitive to stand over a deceased liberal saying, "I bet you wish you had heeded Pat Robertson's hurricane warnings now," or, "Let's see if that affirmative action plan helps get you into heaven now."

What to Do If You're Sleeping with the Enemy

"Well, there was no sex for fourteen days."
    —ex-California Governor Arnold Schwarzenegger, on how his wife, Maria Shriver (of Kennedy clan fame), reacted after he gave a speech praising President Bush at the 2004 Republican Convention. (Years later, when he admitted to fathering a love child with the family maid, he earned himself a lifetime sex ban.)

Love makes people do crazy things, and chief among them is dating (or even marrying) your political enemy. Many households have their own partisan divides. He listens to Rush Limbaugh; she listens to NPR. He votes for the candidate he'd like to drink beer with; she goes with the person she'd rather trust performing brain surgery. He's James Carville, the serpent-headed Democratic strategist known as the Ragin' Cajun; she's Mary Matalin, the sharp-tongued Republican strategist who helped Dick Cheney rule the galaxy.

Some mixed couples manage to coexist in a state of harmony. For others, it ends with a restraining order. Consider the case of one couple in Georgia who made headlines after the woman informed her boyfriend, a Marine recruit, that she was leaving him *and* voting for John Kerry back in 2004. That's when he tried to stab her repeatedly with a screwdriver. "You'll never live to see the election," he told her before officers subdued him with a Taser.

To help you remain faithful to both your beliefs and your significant other (while keeping yourself out of jail), here are a few pointers.

★ **DO** tease your significant other about how she is really a Republican deep down. (How else to explain the Schwarzenegger DVD collection or the fact that Senator Scott Brown is on her celebrity sex list?)

★ **DO** consider withholding sex to make a political point. If that doesn't work, women can try withholding gadgets or restricting his PlayStation or TiVo privileges. (Note: This suggestion may be an impossible task for males to pull off. Only make these threats if you are absolutely certain you can go through with it. If you are bluffing, your bluff will be called! Expect your female partner to look hotter than she has ever looked and offer to do things to you sexually that you are going to have to Google. All this while she's unboxing the latest *Call of Duty* game.)

★ **DO** compromise; if she insists on listening to NPR while you're driving around, put a "Stop Global Whining" bumper sticker on the car.

★ **DO** agree on a safe word to signal when you've reached your limit, like people do with S&M; if he's extolling the virtues of repealing the capital gains tax and you just can't take it anymore, shout out "eight ball," "bananas," or "Bernanke" and take a time-out.

★ **DON'T** engage in any sort of political discussion with your opposite-ideological partner if you're hoping to get laid afterward. Wait until after sex. Two and a half minutes is not going to kill you. Remember, if you're having sex correctly, you won't have the energy for the argument to get out of hand. (If perchance the sex was unprotected, now would be a good time to discuss your opposition to abortion.)

★ **DON'T** resort to amateurish passive aggressive behavior, such as lining the birdcage with your honey's absentee ballot. Instead, take it up a notch—host an NRA party and use her old Barbra Streisand LPs for skeet shooting.

★ **DON'T** let resentments fester; if you're still bitter about the volunteer work she did for the Al Sharpton 2004 presidential campaign, it's time to let it go. If anything, she deserves your pity.

★ **DON'T** kid yourself; if you discover a tote bag containing baggy fatigues, a crowbar, a gas mask, and a bundle of anti-Wall-Street leaflets, pack up the kids and head for the nearest red state. You should also disavow any knowledge of your partner because she is about to be "occupying" the back of a paddy wagon.

★   **DON'T** hold discussions, arguments, or brawls around knives, cutlery, or sharp objects. You may think you won the argument, only to wake up Bobbitted, and that's one cut neither party should support.

How to Manage Workplace Squabbles

During the course of their adult lives, most Americans are doomed to spend about one-third of their waking hours toiling in the workplace. Whether you're looking for a political argument or not, sooner or later you're bound to find yourself mixing it up with that liberal colleague who's whining about the evils of corporate America, totally oblivious to the fact that her job in corporate America pays for her Prius, her Botox, and the braces on her kid's buck teeth.

Because workplace arguments can be a serious occupational hazard, here are some tips that will help you serve your partisan cause while holding onto your job at the same time.

★   **DO** turn a difference of opinion into a friendly wager. If you win a bet about Republicans winning the upcoming election, for example, your coworker has to agree to travel the country following Hank Williams Jr. on tour. If you lose, you agree to follow Phish. *Do not lose*, or else you'll end up smelling like weed and feet.

★ **DO** form alliances with like-minded colleagues; a coordinated assault around the water cooler by a coalition of the willing is always better than going it alone. It will also make that march you have planned on the IT department more effective. If you're marching by yourself, they'll think you're there for IT help, rather than protesting the socialist firewall they created that restricts you from watching Glenn Beck's web TV show at work.

★ **DO** leverage your position to impose your views on others. If you are in the IT department, set office passwords to things like "go_romney," "tax-cutsfortherich!" "chooselife," or "suckit_obama."

★ **DO** consider being a double agent; convince a liberal colleague that you're actually a liberal too and win his or her trust. This may involve doing some unspeakable acts, such as reading Karl Marx's *Das Kapital* or restricting yourself to drinking wheat grass juice for lunch. Then at a crucial moment—say, right before Election Day—express your total disillusionment with the Democratic Party and convince your colleague to join you in abandoning ship.

★ **DON'T** get into a political spat with your boss or anyone else above your pay grade. You will not find any talking points on Fox News that will help you argue against "You're fired!"

★ **DON'T** be a stalker, like that guy in accounting with bad breath who's always cornering people, ranting about which countries should be nuked, and trying to get you to read his MySpace blog; no one likes that guy. That's why they don't tell him MySpace is a dead social network.

★ **DON'T** plaster your workspace with annoying propaganda or signage (e.g., stickers that say "Warning: I'm just a bitter Christian clinging to my gun," "I love Gitmo," or that photo of you patrolling the Mexican border with the Minute Men). It signals you're either desperate for attention or huffing liquid paper. In either case, your coworkers will avoid you.

"They say, 'It's not whether you win or lose, it's how you play the game.' That's why I play every sport with a baseball bat—the other boxer never sees it coming."

—Stephen Colbert

How to Clash with Perfect Strangers

A few days after the 2004 presidential election, a pugnacious liberal posted the following anonymous message on craigslist.org in Washington, D.C.: "I would like to fight a Bush supporter to vent my anger. If you are one, [and] have a fiery streak, please contact me so we can meet and physically fight. I would like to beat the shit out of you."

Another craigslist poster offered a similar proposition: "Any of you Republicans want to fight? Street brawl, bodies only, no weapons. I will not be merciful. I'm sick of this tough-guy shit. Let's see what you got." (While most suspect those ads were posted by Sean Penn, it's clear liberals are an unbalanced lot.)

Going around and picking fights with strangers is generally not recommended. However, there are a few situations where *verbally* mixing it up with strangers may be warranted, perhaps even imperative. Here are a few guidelines.

★ **DO** feel free to mix it up with petition gatherers, pamphleteers, and other partisan stalkers; the longer you hold them hostage, the less time they'll have to disperse their propaganda to others. In fact, take as much paraphernalia as they're willing to hand out to you. Then, when you're closing the door or walking away, say loud enough for them to hear: "This stuff will make great kindling for our next book burning!" or "Hey honey, you can hold off on running to Walmart for toilet paper."

★ **DO** crash Occupy protests and make a point to verbally taunt protesters; if you can provoke an angry, unhinged outburst from just one peace-loving hippie, it will make for amusing news coverage.

★ **DO** feel free to heckle any celebrity performer who decides to launch into an obnoxious anti-Republican tirade while you're sitting in the audience. The next time somebody pulls a Dixie Chick on you, shout them down by saying, "Shut up and play, ya socialist hippie! Isn't that just like a liberal; charge me fifty bucks then force me to listen to failed ideas"; or "If I wanted to hear

forty-five minutes of crap I'd turn on C-SPAN."
If you happen to be carrying lighter fluid for
just such an event, a post-concert CD-burning
bonfire can be a great way to meet new friends.

★ **DON'T** antagonize anyone who may be able to
take advantage of you in a compromising situation, such as your hairstylist, skydiving instruc-
tor, proctologist, tattoo artist, or the guy making
your burrito.

★ **DON'T** get into an argument with the liberal sitting next to you on an airplane. You don't know
what kind of terrorist sympathizer he or she might
be, so it's best not to set them off. Being stuck on
a plane with a crazy person is no fun, especially
when you have no exit strategy.

★ **DON'T** engage in fisticuffs with liberals; they'll
curl into the fetal position before you can even
land a punch, and then slap you with a lawsuit
claiming emotional distress. They're a lot like
the French, only more litigious.

How to Argue Politics on Facebook and Twitter

Popular social media sites like Facebook and Twitter have done more than just revolutionize the way we stalk old flames or tend to virtual crops; they've also pioneered entirely new ways to win or lose political arguments.

You're bound to have at least a few hardcore liberals among your friends or followers, which means sooner or later you're going to see the unwelcome sight of someone pasting some "Occupy" babble about aborting same-sex immigrant entitlements, or re-Tweeting pleas for campaign donations for Elizabeth Warren. Butting heads through these kinds of social media interactions (in what amounts to a room full of all your friends) is fraught with great danger, but also great opportunity, which is why some unique DOs and DON'Ts apply.

★ **DO** enlist other Facebook friends to engage in a virtual sneak attack. You can start the fun by updating your status with provocative statements that will drive your opponents crazy, like "Obama's neo-socialist wealth redistributionist ideology is destroying the economy. Use those tax dollars to buy a clue. At least Jimmy Carter could run a peanut farm." If a liberal takes the bait, privately message your friends and get them to swarm on him like wild dogs on a piece of meat. By the time he's finished reading the tenth successive post illustrating why he's both wrong and an idiot, he'll never know what hit him.

★ **DO** create intentionally misleading Twitter identities for evil liberals like @Olbermannia, @fancynancyP_SF, @GaffmeisterVP, @dirtyharryreid, @SorosConspiracies, @commradBernieSanders, @RachelMadcow, or @KenyanBarryBPrez, and then post things that are closer to the truth than the actual fluff they post. For instance: "@ KenyanBarryBprez: hired new caddy today, who says I can't make jobs? LMFAO! #occupy countryclubs"; "@GaffmiesterVP: Secret Service guys hate when you do doughnuts in rose garden. FML"; and "@Olbermannia: Help! Stuck on network with even smaller viewership than MSNBC, who knew that was possible?"

★ **DO** feel free to tweet outlandish statements about your opponents, as long as you follow it up with the hashtag "justsaying" (#justsaying). This absolves you of any responsibility for whatever you attribute to that individual because you were "justsaying" that. So if you say: "Nancy Pelosi moonlights in lucrative career scaring birds in cornfield #justsayin", or "Joe Biden's tramp stamp is Chinese character for class warrior #justsaying," or "Obama's new jobs bill includes $40 billion subsidy for pimping #justsaying," then your opponent can't get mad at you because you remembered to use the #justsaying hashtag.

★ **DON'T** take the bait when somebody you know on Facebook attempts to get a rise out of his righty friends by spewing so called "facts" about conservatives trying to poison the environment, destroy the middle class, or execute the mentally challenged. If his post is met with crickets, not only will he look like a loser, he'll also be punished by Facebook's algorithm for failing to elicit interaction, and fewer and fewer people will see his posts over time. You win by silence and by default. God bless Mark Zuckerberg.

★ **DON'T** "like" your own posts or comments. It just makes you look like an insecure egomaniac or an idiot who hit the wrong button. Instead, create a fake account, and then you'll have your own personal wingman who can like everything you say, and post fawning comments such as "You are SO insightful," "You go girl!" or "LOL! This is the funniest comparison of Obama's jobs bill and Anthony Weiner's junk. Funny and scary!"

★ **DON'T** pay to have millions of fake Twitter followers and then brag about them as your credential for being president. (See Gingrich, Newt)

★ **DON'T** use cutesy lingo like IMHO (in my humble opinion) on Twitter. If you say it, we know it's your opinion, and if you are broadcasting it on Twitter, it's probably not sincerely humble. Also avoid LOL or LMAO at your own Tweets—we'll be the judge of that, thank you. In real life if you have to laugh out loud at your own jokes to let people know they're funny, you just look like a moron.

★ **DON'T** unfriend, block, or completely hide the updates from your crazy lefty friends, because you'll be missing out the chance to bait and mock them. Instead, create a special list for these people. Call it something like "Monkeys in a Barrel." Think of it as you own private window to the loony bin. Check it periodically to see how the Left is "thinking," or to test out new lines of attack. Or, if you're having a crappy day, just rip into them. It's twenty-four-hour free cathartic therapy, and about the only affordable health care liberals will ever give you.

★ **DON'T** drink and tweet. When you come home after a long night of revelry, it may be tempting to respond to a left-wing jab, but don't do it. You won't be at your sharpest and it undermines your credibility when you Tweet things like "Build electric border fence but let in Jose Cuervo" or "Bachmann-Palin would be a good ticket but better three-way" or "New weird rash definitely not covered by Obamacare." Remember, Twitter is a public medium and once you press "send," it's out there. You don't want to wake up in the morning to find that your response to a tweet on the validity of Keynesian economics was a two-word tweet that said "suck it," accompanied by an uncensored photo of your junk.

How to Properly Engage in Internet Flame Wars

If you've never been denounced as a bedwetting, fascist, crack-addicted, terrorist crybaby by dozens of people you've never met, you've never experienced the joys of an Internet flame war. For the uninitiated, here's a recap of every political debate ever held in an online political forum or the comments section of various blogs and news sites, courtesy of Bill Maher:

"'Obama is a socialist.' 'Oh yeah, Bush is a war criminal, fag.' 'Who you calling a fag, faggot?' The end. And then of course, someone chimes in with 'Ron Paul 2012,' and they call that guy a fag. And then, I can't help myself, so I type, 'Gentlemen, gentlemen, please! This is a porn site!'"

The upside to engaging in Internet flame wars is (1) you get to deploy all the anti-liberal epithets and denunciations that have been swirling in your mind (see After-*Words*: 125,000 Ways to Insult Liberals); and (2) it's generally all anonymous, which means there's no need to lose any sleep over the taunts or fatwas that will inevitably be issued against you.

If you plan to get involved in a flame war, here are a few things to keep in mind. Note that some of these tips run counter to the advice offered elsewhere in the book. That's the whole point of flame wars. They're anonymous, so normal rules of decorum need not apply.

★   **DO** tell anyone who calls you a Nazi that they've automatically lost the argument for violating Godwin's Law of Nazi Analogies, which says that in any sufficiently long Internet discussion, someone will eventually compare his or her opponent to Nazis or Hitler. Be sure to make this point while calling your opponent everything short of a Nazi (i.e., digital brownshirt, cyber jihadist, fascist troll, and, where appropriate, batshit-crazy, genocidal douche bag).

★ **DO** feel free to invent your own facts. If pressed for evidence, simply create your own Wikipedia entry to support your made-up arguments. The Internet is overflowing with incorrect information; what's a little more going to hurt?

★ **DO** occasionally misrepresent yourself to play mind games with your opponent. You're no longer a conservative who wants to cut taxes for job creators. You're now a liberal economics professor who supports the idea. You're no longer a conservative who believes in intelligent design. You're now a Nobel Prize-winning scientist who believes only a divine hand could have created Eva Mendes, the iPad, and Cool Ranch Doritos. You're no longer a conservative who believes Obama was born in Kenya. You're now one of his Kenyan cousins who has the placenta to prove it.

★ **DO** keep your posts concise. If your comment is longer than the initial article, your opponents will immediately dismiss you as a latter-day Unabomber. Remember, while brevity is the soul of wit, long-windedness is the soul of a forty-year-old living in his parents' garage.

★ **DO** take personal offense to everything you can, even if it's not personal. Explain, for example, that you lost an arm, a leg, and an eye in the War on Christmas and you're outraged by his callous insensitivity. Tell him that somewhere terrorists are reading his posts and high-fiving each other because they know they've won.

★ **DO** pretend to be an expert on whatever subject matter you're arguing, as a way of pulling rank and trumping your opponent. If you're arguing about illegal immigration, say you're a border security guard. If you're arguing about terrorism, say you're a member of Seal Team 6. If you're arguing about the environment, tell them you're Al Gore. If they ask how you got on their Mommy's Group discussion thread, remind them you invented the Internet.

★ **DO** demonstrate that you are on the cutting edge of Internet discourse by using expletives such as "asshat," "derp," and "dill weed." Bonus points: If you use the number "3" instead of the letter "e" and "P" in place of "O," you'll confuse the piss out of them and let them know they've been "Pwn3d! LOL!"

★ **DON'T** ever defend your own arguments. That's a rookie mistake and a waste of your time. Instead, keep your opponent constantly on the defensive. For example, after you've stated that liberals want to bring grandma before a death panel, don't respond to their demands for proof; simply move on to your next attack, arguing that JFK was a notorious cross-dresser. Put the onus on them to disprove everything you're saying. If they hit Caps Lock and start shouting at you, consider that a win. You have helped create a safe outlet for their rage, and that's one less kitten they're likely to torture.

★ **DON'T** ever provide any real information about yourself. Facebook is doing enough of that already and you don't need any more personal info on the Internet. Besides, it's more fun to pretend to be someone you're not—a mid-level Homeland Security official, for example, who is carefully monitoring everything they're saying.

★ **DON'T** get overly worked up or spend too much time flaming. You are never going to "win" the argument. In the annals of Internet flame wars, not once has anyone walked away from the computer saying, "You know, righty69 made a good point. Keynesian economics has proven ineffective and perhaps it is time we try a supply-side approach." The goal is not to "win"; it's to make the other guy as angry as possible. If you get angry or worked up, you lose.

★ **DON'T** limit yourself to just one identity, make sure to have several. The more the merrier. Use an entire online ensemble to agree with you and trash your opponent. It may feel a little like cheating, but if your opponent thinks the entire Internet is run by conservatives, it may keep him off the Internet and out of your life.

CHAPTER 6

Kick-Ass Comebacks to Liberal Nonsense

"Yeah, well, you know, that's just, like, uh, your opinion, man."

—The Dude in *The Big Lebowski*.

Always bet on The Dude.

Now that you're primed for battle, it's time to get down and dirty and argue the issues. Liberals mindlessly spew so many ludicrous talking points that are unsupported by facts and common sense, it's hard to rebut them all. But we present here a bundle of kick-ass comebacks to common left-wing ridiculousness you're likely to encounter.

Your goal is to seize control and reframe the debate to your advantage through all necessary means: throw inconvenient facts in their faces, stump them with pointed questions, expose their ignorance, beat them in a battle of wits, or quote somebody famous or funny to help make your point.

Keep in mind there's no such thing as a magical retort that will leave your opponent flattened as you triumphantly spike the ball in the end zone. But think of these as winning openers that will put you in a better position to win—or at least temporarily shut them up as they scramble to pull more drivel from the shallow recesses of their bong-resin-clogged brains.

How to Argue with Mindless Obama Lovers

When they say: America is better off now than it was four years ago.

You say: Right, employment is booming, and the deficit is under control, the war in Afghanistan is going great, I can levitate, and if you don't believe me, just ask my unicorn.

When they say: Obama has helped the economy.

You say: Obama has had the worst jobs record of any U.S. president since World War II. Unemployment soared after he took office and remained abysmal through most of his first term. So I don't think "helped the economy" means what you think it means.

When they say: Obama inherited Bush's economy and financial meltdown.

You say: Obama might want to update his Teleprompter because he's been blaming Bush since 2004. After three years and $4.5 trillion dollars in additional spending, regardless of where you started, you have to own up to your lack of progress. Liberals love to point fingers and play the blame game. And that makes sense because you know what blame and liberals have in common? Neither provides any solutions.

When they say: You guys had eight years to kill Osama bin Laden and Obama got it done in less than three.

You say: Kudos on that, but when you are done congratulating yourselves, you might want to take note that Iran has or is about to have nuclear weapons. Do you want to bet they'd pass those off to Hamas or Al Qaeda? That's the problem with liberals, you just don't get that this is a war on terror, not a police raid on some kids that knocked over a liquor store.

When they say: Obama won a Nobel Peace Prize.

You say: So did fellow Muslim Yasser Arafat and fellow failed President Jimmy Carter. I think the AARP is more selective.

When they say: Obama kept us from going into a depression, and he'll lead us out of this recession if we just give him another four years.

You say: Obama's policies have done for the economy what gasoline has done for fire. The national debt is at $15 trillion and has increased almost $4.5 trillion since Obama took office. Add the looming costs of his policies like Obamacare and the unprecedented increase in job-killing regulation, and you'll find what's really depressing is the prospect that this over-matched nitwit might get a second term.

When they say: Things could have been a lot worse if it weren't for Obama's policies.

You say: So you guys went from "hope" and "change" to "it could have been worse." That's a triumphant slogan. Better go put that on a bumper sticker. That's like the *Titanic* lobbying for a second voyage after boasting that not everyone drowned.

When they say: At least Obama is popular in the rest of the world, so he must be doing something right.
You say: Of course he's popular overseas. That's where he's created all the jobs.

When they say: Obama is a strong leader.
You say: Strong? He makes Jimmy Carter look like FDR. But don't take my word for it. Take one of your own. James Carville said, "If Hillary gave up one of her balls and gave it to Obama, he'd have two."

When they say: Obama is an inspirational speaker.
You say: So was Jim Jones.

Bart Simpson: *"Didn't you wonder why you were getting checks for doing absolutely nothing?"*
Grandpa Simpson: *"I figured 'cause the Democrats were in power again."*

—*The Simpsons*

How to Argue with Economic Ignoramuses

When they say: We need the government to provide more economic stimulus.

You say: Here's one of the main differences between the Left and Right: Conservatives trust working Americans to spend their money more wisely than Barack Obama or Nancy Pelosi can. When people have more cold cash in hand, it spurs investment, creates jobs, boosts the economy, and benefits everyone—with the one exception being the drum circle industry (with everyone working, who's going to man the drums?). We tried your stimulus plan and it failed spectacularly! Obama predicted his stimulus would keep unemployment under 8 percent. Well, it hit 10 percent and has been stuck around 9 for most of his term. But he did manage to add $789 billion to the budget deficit. And that's change we can all count on... not getting back.

When they say: Corporations are not people.
You say: Everyone who works at a corporation *is a person*!

When they say: I am the 99%.

You say: "I work three jobs. I have a house I can't sell. My family insurance costs are outrageous. But I don't blame Wall Street. Suck it up, you whiners. I am the 53% subsidizing you so you can hang out on Wall Street and complain." —*Erick Erickson, editor of Redstate.com*

When they say: Conservatives believe the answer to everything is to cut taxes.

You say: Well, we wouldn't have to keep cutting them if liberals would stop raising them. Seriously, the government beast is out of control, and the more you feed it, the bigger it gets. We're just trying to put government on a diet, and no one can argue Americans don't need a diet.

When they say: We should all be paying higher taxes.

You say: If you feel so virtuous about it, why wait for a tax hike? Why don't you set an example and send a check for a few extra thousand dollars to the federal government? I'm sure your money will be well spent. Maybe they'll buy some new gold-plated hub caps for Obama's million-dollar campaign bus.

"Any rich man does more for society than all the jerks pasting 'Visualize World Peace' bumper stickers on their cars. The worst leech of a merger and acquisitions lawyer making $500,000 a year will, even if he cheats on his taxes, put $100,000 into the public coffers. That's $100,000 worth of education, charity, or U.S. Marines. And the Marine Corps does more to promote world peace than all the Ben & Jerry's ice cream ever made."

—P. J. O'Rourke

When they say: Unemployment insurance is vital in a bad economy.

You say: Reagan put it best when he said, "Unemployment insurance is a pre-paid vacation for freeloaders." When the government creates more incentive for the unemployed to sit around smoking weed and eating Pork Rinds than there is to go out and get a job, guess what you end up with? High unemployment and a lot of stoned, flabby, social welfare parasites.

When they say: Liberals are the ones who stick up for the little guy.

You say: If you ask me, the guy taking my wallet is not

sticking up for me; he's sticking me up. That's like the Mafia saying its collection policies protect small business owners from broken legs. At least the Mafia doesn't break their own arms patting themselves on the back about what good and moral people they are for stealing the fruits of your labor.

When they say: Corporate fat cats are buying off Republicans and corrupting politics.

You say: "I've never been able to understand why a Republican contributor is a 'fat cat' and a Democratic contributor of the same amount of money is a 'public-spirited philanthropist." —*Ronald Reagan*

When they say: Conservatives are in bed with big business.

You say: Like using taxpayer money to gamble in the energy market on a company whose chief investor is a big contributor to your party? Oh wait, that was Obama with $535 million dollars in loan guarantees to Solyndra. You might not want to throw stones from your solar glass house.

When they say: Republicans and the Tea Party held the country hostage when they failed to raise the debt ceiling.

You say: Actually, liberals were holding America's credit card hostage and conservatives were trying to get it back. At this rate each American family is responsible for $130,000 in debt. Every day we fail to rein in the national debt and radically cut spending means a larger burden that we pass on to our children.

When they say: Conservatives hate the poor because they are always trying to cut welfare and entitlements.

You say: I'll let a revered former president answer this one: "Continued dependence upon relief induces a spiritual and moral disintegration fundamentally destructive to the national fiber. To dole out relief in this way is to administer a narcotic, a subtle destroyer of the human spirit." Reagan? Nope, FDR.

"Liberals are generous with other people's money, except when it comes to questions of national survival, when they prefer to be generous with other people's freedom and security."

—**William F. Buckley Jr.**

How to Clash with Clueless Liberals on Hot-Button Issues

When they say: I believe global warming is real.

You say: "From now on, every time somebody tells me they believe in global warming, I can say to them, 'So you agree with Charles Manson.'" —*Stephen Colbert*

When they say: Conservatives hate the environment.

You say: No, conservatives just aren't screaming the sky is falling based on inconclusive data and incomplete science. Conservatives particularly want to protect an endangered species called job creators. Because of the EPA, Job Creationist-Americans are moving their jobs, manufacturing, and energy production to other countries like China, which have little if any concern for protecting the environment. And sadly, pollution has no respect for international borders. But I guess on the bright side, not having jobs and living in the street will give us more time to enjoy the newly saved giant pygmy squirrel.

When they say: Conservatives are anti-immigrant.

You say: Conservatives are anti-*illegal* immigrant. Conservatives welcome any individual who follows the rules and does the due diligence to partake in the American dream. We hope they bring their creative ideas, energy, and tasty foods, and we welcome them to the melting pot. But for illegal aliens trying to sneak into this country at great expense to the taxpayers, we'd like to introduce you to our friends, predator drone and electrical fence.

When they say: Conservatives are all a bunch of gun nuts.

You say: Considering the fact that we're packing, we'd prefer you use the term "firearm enthusiasts." Seriously, it's in the Bill of Rights, just after free speech. It's a slippery slope when you start curtailing individual freedom. I wouldn't advise you try it, unless you feel lucky. Well, do you, punk?

When they say: Health-care reform will bring down costs.

You say: "If you think health care is expensive now, wait until you see what it costs when it's free." —P.J. O'Rourke

When they say: What's so bad about government-run health-care?

You say: "If you put the federal government in charge

of the Sahara Desert, in five years there'd be a shortage of sand." —*Milton Friedman*

When they say: Making everyone get health insurance is better for the country.

You say: How is taking away my freedom of choice making this country better? I'm pretty sure this is how the Soviet Union got started.

When they say: The Occupy Wall Street movement is just like the Tea Party movement, only better.

You say: Really? The Occupy movement has had more violent crime, robberies, and arrests than any Tea Party rally. Also, I'm pretty sure Tea Party members didn't take a dump on any police cars.

When they say: Conservatives want to fire teachers and cut education.

You say: Conservatives do want to fire teachers, the bad ones. The ones who are letting American children fall further and further behind the rest of the world. Conservatives want to get rid of the huge federal educational bureaucracy that eats up resources and could be better spent in the classroom. Conservatives want to introduce proven free-market solutions like competition and choice into the school system. Liberals sleep better knowing more money is being spent on education. Conservatives sleep better knowing more children are being educated.

When they say: Conservatives are anti-union.

You say: Conservatives are pro-individual, and since Democrats and liberals are on the Big Union payroll, it's up to conservatives to protect the rights of individuals. When it's labor vs. liberty, for conservatives it's an easy call.

When they say: Conservatives are in denial about teen sexuality, and abstinence is not the answer.

You say: We're not in denial. We're just seeking a moral counterbalance from the media. Kids are getting their sexual values from the Kardashian sisters and *Jersey Shore*. Our schools only teach teens how to avoid diseases and not get pregnant. They don't give kids the moral compass to abstain from sex or teach the realities of being a teenage single parent. I think all Americans can agree, the last thing we need is a generation of sexual Snookies.

When they say: I support abortion rights.

You say: "I've noticed that everyone that is for abortion has already been born." —*Ronald Reagan*

When they say: Conservatives want to destroy the social safety net.

You say: Conservatives think it's ridiculous to be paying a dollar for a nickel's worth of services. Social Security is an unsustainable Ponzi scheme, while Medicare and Medicaid are facing skyrocketing costs with no end in sight. Conservatives want to give states and individuals the right to make more decisions about their health care and retirement. We can all agree we don't want bureaucrats who think we should pay $15 for a muffin or $400 for a hammer making those decisions for our families.

When they say: Conservatives are trying to dismantle the EPA and FDA.

You say: Regulators like the EPA and FDA are trying to dismantle the U.S. economy. Regulations sound nice, but the truth is every new regulation costs Americans jobs and consumers a hidden tax in the form of higher prices. In 2010, new regulations cost the economy $26.5 billion while total regulations cost $2 trillion. We all want clean air and safe medicine, but adding excessive regulations year after year means the only thing we'll be producing in America is "Out of Business" signs.

When they say: Banks should be punished for selling those bad mortgages.

You say: What about the idiots who signed them? Whatever happened to personal responsibility? The mortgages weren't all bad; people just got in over their heads. You don't go to a fancy restaurant when you know you only have $2 in your pocket, eat a huge meal, and then beg people to help you out. That's called stealing.

When they say: No war for oil.

You say: "Why not go to war just for oil? We need oil. What do Hollywood celebrities imagine fuels their private jets? How do they think their cocaine is delivered to them?" —*Ann Coulter*

"The Occupy movement starts with the premise that we all owe them everything. They take over a public park they didn't pay for, to go nearby to use bathrooms they didn't pay for, to beg for food from places they don't want to pay for, to obstruct those who are going to work to pay the taxes to sustain the bathrooms and to sustain the park, so they can self-righteously explain they are the paragons of virtue to which we owe everything. That is a pretty good symptom of how much the Left has collapsed as a moral system in this country, and why you need to reassert something by saying to them, 'Go get a job right after you take a bath.'"

—Newt Gingrich

How to Rebut Other Liberal Drivel

When they say: What's wrong with socialism?

You say: "The problem with socialism is that eventually you run out of other people's money."
—*Margaret Thatcher*

When they say: Capitalism is the source of our problems.

You say: If I had a dollar for every time capitalism was blamed for the problems created by government, I'd be a fat filmmaker with a baseball hat. *(seen on a bumper sticker)*

When they say: Government can be better trusted to run things than the private sector.

You say: You know what Obama once said when he was trying to make the case for government-run health care? In a rare candid moment without a Teleprompter, he said, "UPS and FedEx are doing just fine, right? It's the Post Office that's always having problems." If even your president can acknowledge that the private sector can get the job done better than government, who are you to argue with him?

When they say: Government isn't all bad. Government does good things.

You say: "Feeling good about government is like looking on the bright side of any catastrophe. When you quit looking on the bright side, the catastrophe is still there." —P.J. O'Rourke

When they say: Liberals believe in innovation and positive change.

You say: "If Thomas Edison had invented the electric light in the age of the welfare state, the Democrats would immediately introduce a bill to protect the candle-making industry." —*Newt Gingrich*

When they say: Conservatives are against progress.

You say: If you define progress as raising taxes on American families, regulating the free market to death, infecting our children with Hollywood morality, and ensuring that every abortion-seeking illegal immigrant has a right to medicinal marijuana, then yes, conservatives are against "progress," and proudly so.

When they say: Conservatives are only out for themselves.

You say: You say that like it's a bad thing. Our country was founded on the idea of promoting individual liberty. Conservatives believe everyone should have equal opportunity to make a buck and be happy—without being made to feel guilty about it. As for everyone else, conservatives believe the most compassionate thing we can do is to empower people to pull themselves up by their bootstraps. Liberals believe in handing out free boots, scolding you for putting them on wrong, and then charging you a boot tax.

When they say: Liberals are more tolerant than conservatives.

You say: Let's see: If you oppose affirmative action, liberals will denounce you as a racist. If you believe in taking a strong stand against illegal immigration, you're a xenophobe. If you think marriage should be between a man and a woman, that's homophobic. Anyone who fails to support the liberal agenda gets tarred as bigoted, intolerant, or in the favorite liberal catchall for all of the above: fascist. How's that for tolerance?

When they say: Conservatives are racist.

You say: Huh? Conservatives are the only ones not making race an issue. Conservatives believe it's time to end affirmative action. Liberals are the ones telling you what race or gender deserves college admission or who a company should hire instead of letting that institution choose the most qualified individual, regardless of race, color, or creed.

When they say: We must look to Congress to solve our problems.

You say: "Suppose you were an idiot. And suppose you were a member of Congress. But I repeat myself."
—*Mark Twain*

When they say: Joe Biden gives the White House a lot of experience.

You say: And that experience will come in handy if we need to know which Bon Jovi song to pick at a karaoke bar, or which light beer goes with stuffed-crust pizza, or if they're a greeter short at Walmart.

When they say: Joe Biden has done a great job as a statesman in places like Bosnia, Serbia, and Kosovo

You say: "The White House is calling it 'Operation Keep Biden Away from the Microphones.'" —*Jay Leno*

When they say: Nancy Pelosi was a much better speaker of the house than John Boehner.

You say: I'm pretty sure everybody else disagrees with you since, on her watch, the Democrats got 86'd faster than a Kennedy on dollar-drink night. Boehner does cry more than Pelosi, we'll give you that, but I think that's only because her tear ducts are fused shut from all the surgeries.

When they say: Republicans are crazy people.

You say: Actually, according to a Gallup poll done a few years back, Republicans reported much better mental health than Democrats (58 percent of Republicans compared to 38 percent of Democrats). But really, who could blame you? If my party couldn't govern its way out of a wet paper bag or caved in on every issue, I'd go nuts too.

When they say: Conservatives should really be more civil in their discourse.

You say: I've upped my standards. Now, up yours. *(with apologies to Pat Paulsen)*

CHAPTER 7

The Liberal Hall
of Shame

"I have only ever made one prayer to God, a very short one: 'Oh Lord, make my enemies ridiculous.' And God granted it."

—**Voltaire**

There is so much rampant hypocrisy and idiocy on the Left, it's nearly impossible to keep track of it all. But you can add extra bite to your arguments—and illustrate just how insane the other side is—by calling attention to the inglorious exploits of celebrated liberals.

Fortunately, it's not hard, as you'll see from this

rundown of some of the most prominent liberal sex fiends, morons, and douche bags who have disgraced national politics in recent years—and earned their place in the Liberal Hall of Shame.

The Wing of Sex Fiends, Perverts, and Adulterers

ANTHONY "JUNK MAIL" WEINER

Claim to shame: Former Congressman Anthony Weiner (D-NY) initially vehemently denied tweeting a photo of his junk to a young woman, claiming he couldn't "say with certitude" whether it was, in fact, his wiener. His pathetic explanation that his account had been hacked went limp in the face of stiff evidence. As Weiner battled for his political life, his poll numbers went soft and he had to think long and hard about his future, before ultimately pulling out. Tabloid headlines mocked him mercilessly: "Mounting Pressure on Weiner," "Fall on Your Sword, Weiner," "Weiner Is Shrinking," "He Couldn't Keep It Up," and "Weiner Finally Yanks Himself." It got so bad for Weiner that he even had to call to make an apology to Bill Clinton, who had offici-ated at his wedding. "What?!" Jon Stewart said. "The congressman had a sex scandal and had to apologize to Bill Clinton? For what?! Copyright infringement?"

JOHN "BRECK GIRL" EDWARDS

Claim to shame: Edwards joined a long list of politicians caught having a sexual relationship with a woman not his wife. He joined a smaller list of politicians caught having a child with that woman. He, however, joined an exclusive list of politicians caught having an affair with a woman not his wife, when his wife happened to be dying of cancer. Upon being confronted by a *National Enquirer* reporter at the Beverly Hills Hilton after paying a late-night visit to his mistress and their child, Edwards did what any self-respecting ex-senator and presidential aspirant with nothing to hide would do—he fled into a bathroom and tried to hold the door shut. Edwards later fessed up to the affair, but continued to deny their love child was his, until finally being shamed to admitting it after he said he could no longer look at himself in the mirror (which, according to Jimmy Fallon, actually freed up "an extra four hours a day for him"). Edwards was later indicted on a host of charges related to spending nearly $1 million to keep his mistress in hiding during his 2008 presidential bid. "Apparently he spent money on everything except condoms," quipped Jay Leno.

ELIOT SPITZER (SPITZER, I BARELY KNOW HER!)

Claim to shame: Considered a rising star in the Democratic Party, the former New York governor also had a rise for prostitutes supplied by The Emperors Club VIP. He came to power as a sanctimonious crusader against ethics violations and corruption, and had also famously busted prostitution rings, apparently so he could keep them all for himself. Commenting on some of the unseemly details about the scandal, *Saturday Night Live*'s Seth Meyers said, "You wanted to have sex with a hooker, but you didn't want to wear a condom? Really? That might not be scary if you were client number one, but you were client number nine. Really? I wear a condom if I'm ninth in line at the deli." Prior to his resignation, Spitzer apologized during a press conference with his wife standing by his side, "apparently, to make sure there was no prostitute under the podium," joked Amy Poehler on SNL.

ERIC "THE GROPER" MASSA

Claim to shame: First, there was "Tickle Me Elmo," then there was "Tickle Me Massa." The disgraced Democratic congressman from New York was forced to resign after several male staffers complained that he made unwanted sexual advances, including one who said Massa groped him. Massa "defended" himself by saying, "Not only did I grope him, I tickled him until he couldn't breathe and four guys jumped on top of me. It was my fiftieth birthday." That was only the second most ridiculous statement he made in his defense. When asked if he was homosexual, Massa refused to answer the question directly, but did tell the reporter to "ask the ten thousand sailors I served with in the Navy." As Seth Meyers said on *Saturday Night Live*, "When crafting a sentence denying your homosexuality, try to leave out phrases like 'ten thousand guys' or names of Village People songs like 'In the Navy.' You might as well have said, 'I'm not gay. Just ask the fellas down at the YMCA."

KWAME KILPATRICK, SEXTING MAYOR

Claim to shame: Elected mayor of Detroit in 2001, Kilpatrick created a trail of corruption and scandals so long and in such a short amount of time that other Democrats view him with awe and wonder. Years after being forced out of office, he's still facing charges of extortion, bribery, fraud, and racketeering—and that's after already pleading guilty to obstruction of justice and serving four months in jail after he lied at a civil trial to cover up an extramarital affair with his chief of staff. The affair was exposed through a series of explicit text messages, which as Jay Leno joked at the time, "was the most embarrassing thing to happen to a Democratic politician in, like, a week." Kilpatrick remained defiant upon resigning, proclaiming, "I want to tell you, Detroit, that you done set me up for a comeback." So look for him to be a Democratic presidential contender when he's eligible for parole.

BILL CLINTON, CIGAR AFICIONADO

Claim to shame: The chatter began in the national media almost the same day Clinton announced his candidacy for president. There was a list of women as long as his Slick Willie with whom he allegedly had done the Arkansas two-step, forming a veritable conga line to make their accusations ("bimbo eruptions," as one of his aides called them). Then came Monica Lewinsky, the twenty-five-year-old White House intern who brought him pizza and flashed her thong. Next thing you know, the chatter was all about a cigar, a blue dress with an inappropriate stain, and an independent counsel report that read like *Penthouse*'s letters to the editor. Clinton vehemently insisted he "did not have sexual relations with that woman" and came up with creative ways to perjure himself while inventing new definitions for the word "is." But he hadn't counted on Lewinsky being an avid collector of dried semen-covered apparel (in her grand jury testimony, she tried to explain it by saying, "It could have been spinach dip or something"). Needless to say, the Clinton-Lewinsky affair will forever remain the sex scandal by which all future Washington sex scandals will be judged (and the standard by which all future lying, philandering, justice-obstructing Democratic presidents will also be impeached). It takes special talent to degrade your office and your marriage in that kind of spectacular fashion. As Dennis Miller put it, "If Bill Clinton were any more low rent, he'd be a spring-break destination."

JESSE "WHO'S YOUR DADDY" JACKSON

Claim to shame: He may have never held a real job, but Reverend Jackson has long held himself up as the personification of liberal moral superiority. This is why it was especially rich when he fathered a child out of wedlock. Better still, he knocked up his mistress while he was ministering to Bill Clinton during the Monica Lewinsky affair. The scandal gave "clearer meaning to the Rainbow Coalition's Operation 'Push,'" quipped Jon Stewart.

DAVID "TIGGER" WU

Claim to shame: Not content to drive half of his congressional staff away by dressing up in a children's tiger costume and emailing photos to them in the middle of the night, the fifty-six-year-old Democratic representative from Oregon decided that "Wuuing" the eighteen-year-old daughter of a longtime friend and having "an unwanted sexual encounter" would prove to everyone that he was mentally stable. "What is it with these Democrats?" asked Jay Leno. "If it's not Weiner's wiener, it's Wu's wang. What is going on?"

JIM MCGREEVEY, TRUCKER TEMPTRESS

Claim to shame: The former New Jersey governor resigned after confessing to carrying on a secret homosexual affair with an Israeli poet. Later, in a tell-all book, McGreevey also recounted how he used to cruise highway rest stops to have anonymous sex with gay truckers. Jay Leno asked the pertinent question: "At what point do you stop having anonymous sex at truck stops and say to yourself, 'I'm tired of this; I'd rather be governor'?"

BARNEY FRANK, PARAGON
OF MASSACHUSETTS VALUES

Claim to shame: The openly gay Massachusetts congress-man hired a gay prostitute he met through a personals ad as a staff member in the 1980s. Frank was reprimanded by the House in 1990 amid revelations that the man was running a prostitution ring out of Frank's apartment. Apparently those are the kinds of values Massachusetts liberals expect their representatives to champion, judg-ing from the 66 percent margin by which they reelected Frank that year. Years later, when he announced his retirement from Congress, Republicans crowed, which struck Jon Stewart as odd. "Losing Barney Frank is the worst thing that could happen to conservatives," he said. "He is the perfect avatar of everything they hate: gay, Jewish, Taxachusetts, arrogant, condescending liberal. He's your everything bagel."

The Wing of Douche Bags
and Morons

ROD "IT'S F**KING GOLDEN!" BLAGOJEVICH

Claim to shame: Former Illinois Gov. Rod Blagojevich was convicted on seventeen counts of corruption for trying to sell President Obama's vacated Senate seat, and one charge of unlawfully imprisoning that thing on his head. Federal prosecutors nailed him after recording a series of profanity-laced conversations in which he said things like "I've got this thing and it's f**king golden," "I'm just not giving it up for f**king nothing," and "Give this motherf**ker Obama his senator? F**k him. For nothing. F**k him." Shocking as it was, Americans were ultimately more shocked by his hair, which has been described by various observers as a perfect bird's nest for some black crows, cotton candy coated with black spray paint, Klingon helmet hair, or something you'd see on *Animal Planet* or *Unsolved Mysteries*. Whatever it is, it remains an innocent victim that is currently serving jail time along with its host body.

CHARLIE "TAX CHEAT" RANGEL

Claim to shame: Convicted of eleven ethics charges and one count of gargling with Drano, the twenty-term New York congressman insisted that the House Ethics Committee (now there's an oxymoron) deprived him of basic legal rights, such as due process, right to counsel, the right to not pay taxes on a villa he owns in the Dominican Republic, and the right to not properly disclose hundreds of thousands of dollars in personal financial assets. Rangel, who had served as Congress's chief tax writer, was eventually censured by the House, stripped of his Ways and Means Committee chairmanship, and, according to humorist Andy Borowitz, was forced to "delete the song 'Hard Out Here for a Pimp' as his ringtone."

ALVIN "FORREST GUMP" GREENE

Claim to shame: Truly, it is the Democrats residing in South Carolina, America's whoopee cushion, who should be ashamed for awarding Greene with the Democratic nomination for the U. S. Senate in 2010. Greene shocked everyone by winning the nomination, despite never holding a campaign event, being unemployed, living with his parents, and facing felony charges for allegedly showing lewd photos to a college student ("I know, sounds like a senator to me," said Jay Leno). Greene's one idea for creating jobs was to have people make action figures in his likeness, and he insisted it was not a joke. Ironically, it may be the most sensible jobs plan any Democrat has recently proposed.

ROBERT "RATSO" RIZZO

Claim to shame: The former city manager of the poverty-stricken town of Bell, California, Robert Rizzo—along with seven other city officials—was arrested for using the town as his own personal piggy bank. Rizzo was the fattest pig at the trough (literally), bringing in over $1.5 million in salary and benefits annually, making him the highest paid public official in the nation, while the average income of the town's mostly Hispanic residents was just under $25,000. Rizzo, a Democrat, was charged with fifty-three counts of misappropriating public funds, but remained unapologetic, joking about getting "fat" off the city and saying, "If that's a number people choke on, maybe I'm in the wrong business. This council has compensated me for the job I've done." Apparently, the "being an asshole" industry is paying well these days.

WILLIAM "COLD CASH" JEFFERSON

Claim to shame: Who could forget the famously corrupt Democratic congressman from New Orleans who was caught on video accepting a bribe and hiding $90,000 in cash in the freezer? He was sentenced to seven years in jail after being found guilty of what the prosecutor described as "the most extensive and pervasive pattern of corruption in the history of Congress." But he may have gotten a bad rap because as Jay Leno noted, he was "the only politician in Washington who actually saved some money." Had Obama named him Treasury

Secretary, this country's finances might currently be a lot better off.

MICHAEL MOORE-ON

Claim to shame: Opinionated, overweight, and oh-so-hated by the Right, documentary filmmaker and pro-vocateur Michael Moore has made a fortune estimated to be near $50 million pontificating ad nauseam about the evils of capitalism and conservatism. From bashing General Motors to his sad and pathetic attempt to con-front the late Charlton Heston in *Bowling for Columbine* to his unmatched ability to twist a story to suit his own agenda, Moore is to hypocrite as whipped cream is to apple pie. To quote former Bush speechwriter Peter Wehner, "Being a left-wing ideologue is bad enough; being an unprincipled one is worse."

PATRICK KENNEDY, UNSAFE AT ANY SPEED

Claim to shame: Proving once again why you should never mix Kennedys with alcohol, Ted Kennedy's son, Patrick, plowed his car into a U.S. Capitol barrier at 3:00 a.m. one night after a drunken bender. The former Rhode Island congressman claimed to a police officer that he was on his way to vote. But as Bill Maher joked, Kennedy really didn't "remember anything about the accident, except a huge sense of relief when he came to and he wasn't soaking wet."

SANDY "BURGLAR" BERGER

Claim to shame: Before testifying to the 9/11 commission, Sandy Berger, Bill Clinton's national security adviser, embarked on a quest to retrieve highly classified documents at the National Archives. Hoping to elude archive officials, he reportedly stuffed several documents into his socks and exited the building. According to his guilty plea, once outside, he hid the documents under a construction trailer. Later, he spirited the documents back to his office, where he cut them up with scissors. When archive officials confronted him about the missing documents, Berger then went on a desperate hunt to find the trash collector, to no avail. As the guy that Clinton put in charge of protecting America during his administration, Berger's escapades proved he was nothing more than the poor man's Indiana Jones.

JAMES "BEAM ME UP" TRAFICANT

Claim to shame: Arguably the nuttiest Democrat ever to serve in Congress, Traficant used to end his colorful floor speeches by saying "beam me up"—until he was thrown in jail for bribery, racketeering, and tax fraud.

He also forced his staff to clean horse stalls on his farm and work on his houseboat. Asked by the House Ethics Committee to explain his need for a houseboat, the Democratic gadfly said, "I wanted to have Playboy bunnies come on at night to meet with me. I wanted to be promiscuous with them." He once vowed that after he got out of jail, he would "grab a sword like Maximus Meridius Demidius, and as a gladiator I will stab people in the crotch." Upon his release seven years later, he made a losing bid to get re-elected, proving that crazy is mightier than the sword.

"The tyrant fears laughter more than the assassin's bullet."

—Robert A. Heinlein

CHAPTER 8

How to Use Liberals' Own Words against Them

"Voters quickly forget what a man says."

—**President Richard Nixon**

One of the best ways to hammer away at liberals is to smear them with their own words.

Here are some handy quotes to keep in your arsenal that you can throw at your opponents when you need examples of left-wing idiocy, derangement, mendacity, or incompetence. Fortunately, there's an almost limitless supply.

Stunningly Moronic Liberal Quotes

"I've now been in fifty-seven states—I think one left to go."

> —then-presidential candidate Barack Obama
> at a 2008 campaign event

"My fear is that the whole island will become so overly populated that it will tip over and capsize."

> —Rep. Hank Johnson (D-GA),
> expressing concern during a congressional hearing
> that the presence of a large number of American
> soldiers might upend the island of Guam

"I mean, you got the first mainstream African American who is articulate and bright and clean and a nice-looking guy. I mean, that's a storybook, man."

> —Joe Biden on Barack Obama while they were
> both campaigning for president in 2007

"Winnie the Pooh seems to me to be a fundamental text on national security."

— Obama foreign policy adviser Richard Danzig

"Millionaire job creators are like unicorns. They're impossible to find, and they don't exist."

—Senate Democratic leader Harry Reid,
arguing that no millionaires create jobs

"This is still the greatest country in the world, if we just will steel our wills and lose our minds."

—President Bill Clinton

"Biking through New York's boroughs in 2005, I thought about some old friends, Joe and Eileen Bailey. Though they are imaginary, I frequently talk to them."

—Sen. Chuck Schumer (D-NY),
writing in his book, *Positively American*

"Look, John [McCain's] last-minute economic plan does nothing to tackle the number-one job facing the middle class, and it happens to be, as Barack says, a three-letter word: jobs. J-O-B-S, jobs."

—Joe Biden

"Today is a big day in America. Only thirty-six thousand people lost their jobs today."

—Senate Democratic leader Harry Reid, taking to the Senate floor to herald a better-than-expected unemployment report showing the economy lost thirty-six thousand jobs in February 2010

"Every month that we do not have an economic recovery package, five hundred million Americans lose their jobs."

—then-House Speaker Nancy Pelosi

"Those who survived the San Francisco earthquake said, 'Thank God, I'm still alive.' But, of course, those who died, their lives will never be the same again."

—Sen. Barbara Boxer (D-CA)

"It's time to put our blood or our urine where our mouth is."

—Iowa state Rep. and House Speaker Pat Murphy (D), on drug testing

"Now that we're on dog pee, we can have an interesting conversation about that. I do not recommend drinking urine…but if you drink water straight from the river, you have a greater chance of getting an infection than you do if you drink urine."

> —former Vermont Gov. and DNC
> Chairman Howard Dean, teaching
> an eighth-grade science class

"Who among us does not love NASCAR?"

> —Sen. John Kerry (D-MA),
> campaigning for president

"You cannot go to a 7-Eleven or a Dunkin' Donuts unless you have a slight Indian accent…I'm not joking."

> —Joe Biden, in a private remark to an Indian
> American man, which was caught on C-SPAN

"I can't say with certitude. My system was hacked. Pictures can be manipulated, pictures can be dropped in and inserted."

> —former Rep. Anthony Weiner (D-NY),
> when asked whether a lewd Twitter picture
> of him actually showed his wiener

"It all depends on what the meaning of the word 'is' is."

—Bill Clinton, testifying about
his affair with Monica Lewinsky

"During my service in the United States Congress, I took the initiative in creating the Internet."

—Al Gore

"I'm blacker than Barack Obama. I shined shoes. I grew up in a five-room apartment. My father had a little laundromat in a black community not far from where we lived. I saw it all growing up."

—former Illinois Gov. Rod Blagojevich (D)

"If I were a single man, I might ask that mummy out. That's a good-looking mummy."

—Bill Clinton, on "Juanita,"
a newly discovered Incan mummy on display
at the National Geographic museum

"A zebra does not change its spots."

—Al Gore

"Stand up, Chuck, let 'em see ya."

> —Joe Biden, to Missouri state
> Sen. Chuck Graham, who is in a wheelchair

"Let me be absolutely clear. Israel is a strong friend of Israel's."

> —President Obama

"When I meet with world leaders, what's striking—whether it's in Europe or here in Asia…"

> —President Obama, mistakenly referring to
> Hawaii as Asia while holding a press
> conference outside Honolulu

"It was also interesting to see that political interaction in Europe is not that different from the United States Senate. There's a lot of—I don't know what the term is in Austrian, wheeling and dealing."

> —President Obama, confusing German for
> "Austrian," a language that does not exist

"I know I'm the people's senator, but do I have to hang out with them?"

> —former Sen. John Edwards (D-NC),
> as quoted by a former aide Andrew
> Young in the book *The Politician*

"I am the government."

> —New York Gov. Andrew Cuomo (D),
> on being the government

"Great things happen in small places. Jesus was born in Bethlehem. Jesse Jackson was born in Greenville."

> —Jesse Jackson

"I could care less if someone feels me up."

> — Rep. Jim Moran (D-VA), on the TSA's
> controversial airport security procedures

"Why can't I just eat my waffle?"

> —President Obama, after being
> asked a foreign policy question by
> a reporter while visiting a diner

"We're buying shrimp, guys, come on."
>—President Obama, deflecting questions
on Iraq while vacationing

"Come on! I just answered, like, eight questions."
>—President Obama, exasperated
by reporters after a news conference

"Outside of the killings, Washington has one of the lowest crime rates in the country."
>—Marion Barry, former mayor
of Washington, D.C.

"It was an unidentified flying object, OK? It's, like, it's unidentified."
>—Rep. Dennis Kucinich (D-OH), after being asked
about an account in Shirley MacLain's book that
said Kucinich once had a close encounter with a
UFO while visiting her house in Washington state.
MacLaine wrote that Kucinich "felt a connection
in his heart and heard directions in his mind" as a
triangular craft hovered above him.

Reporter: What did you major in in college?
Sen. Carol Moseley Braun (D-IL), who had just announced she was going to run for president: "I'm going to guess it was political science, but I'm not sure. It might have been history. I'll check. I hadn't thought of that one."

"The reforms we seek would bring greater competition, choice, savings, and inefficiencies to our health-care system."

>—President Obama, in remarks after a
> health-care roundtable with physicians,
> nurses, and health-care providers,
> Washington, D.C., July 20, 2009

"Her skirt was very short, and Josh found himself mesmerized by her perfectly shaped, silken legs with kneecaps that reminded him of golden apples."

>—Sen. Barbara Boxer (D-CA),
> writing in her novel A Time to Run

"I can only impregnate. I can't get pregnant myself."
—Rep. Steve Holland (D-Mississippi)

"My staff tells me not to say this, but I'm going to say it anyway. In the summer because of the heat and high humidity, you could literally smell the tourists coming into the Capitol. It may be descriptive but it's true."

—Senate Democratic leader Harry Reid (D-NV)

"We are in a three-way split decision for third place."

—Sen. Joe Lieberman, then a Democratic presidential candidate, on his fifth-place finish in the 2004 New Hampshire presidential primary

"I enjoy cocaine because it's a fun thing to do. …I enjoy the company of prostitutes for the following reasons: it's a fun thing to do. … If you combine the two together it's probably even more fun."

—former Rep. Robert Wexler (D-Fla.), after being egged on to make those statements during an interview with comedian Stephen Colbert

"Most of us weren't born in America at some point in our lives."

—Howard Dean, former Vermont governor and Democratic National Committee Chairman, on immigration reform

"I actually did vote for the $87 billion, before I voted against it."

>—Sen. John Kerry (D-MA), on voting against a
>military funding bill for U.S. troops in Iraq

"I think with a lifetime appointment to the Supreme Court, you can't play, you know, hide the salami, or whatever it's called."

>—Howard Dean, urging President Bush
>to make public Supreme Court nominee
>Harriet Miers's White House records

"I'm the next president...I'll be thirty-five...just before November, so I was born to be president. I'm the man. I'm the man. I'm the man. Greene's the man. I'm the man. I'm the greatest person ever. I was born to be president. I'm the man, I'm the greatest individual ever."

>—failed South Carolina Democratic Senate
>candidate Alvin Greene, on being Alvin Greene

"I'm not going to have some reporters pawing through our papers. We are the president."

>—then-First Lady Hillary Clinton,
>on releasing subpoenaed documents

"A man I'm proud to call my friend. A man who will be the next president of the United States—Barack America!"

> —then-vice presidential candidate Joe Biden,
> at his first campaign rally with Barack Obama
> after being announced as his running mate

"It's always bad practice to say 'always' or 'never.'"

> —President Obama

"When did ignorance become a point of view?"
—Dilbert

Ridiculous, Outrageous, and Delusional Liberal Quotes

"I think when you spread the wealth around, it's good for everybody."

> —then-presidential candidate Barack Obama,
> defending his tax plan to Joe the Plumber,
> who argued that Obama's policy hurts
> small-business owners like himself

"We have to pass the bill so that you can find out what is in it, away from the fog of the controversy."

—then-House Speaker Nancy Pelosi,
talking about health-care reform

"We are going to take things away from you on behalf of the common good."

—then-Sen. Hillary Clinton (D-NY),
on raising taxes

"Guess what this liberal would be all about? This liberal will be about socializing…uh, um…Would be about, basically, taking over, and the government running all of your companies."

—Rep. Maxine Waters (D-CA)

"The conventional viewpoint says we need a jobs program and we need to cut welfare. Just the opposite! We need more welfare and fewer jobs."

—California Gov. Jerry Brown

"We know that no one person can succeed unless everybody else succeeds."

—Howard Dean

"The Republican health-care plan: don't get sick … The Republicans have a backup plan in case you do get sick…This is what the Republicans want you to do. If you get sick, America, the Republican health-care plan is this: die quickly!"

—former Rep. Alan Grayson (D-FL)

"I love these members; they get up and say, 'Read the bill'…What good is reading the bill if it's a thousand pages and you don't have two days and two lawyers to find out what it means after you read the bill?"

—Rep. John Conyers (D-MI),
on the health-care reform bill

"If you love me, you've got to help me pass this bill."

—President Obama on his jobs bill, after an audience member at a North Carolina rally shouted out "I love you!"

"Politics gives guys so much power that they tend to behave badly around women. And I hope I never get into that."

—Bill Clinton

"I have to confess that it's crossed my mind that you could not be a Republican and a Christian."

—Hillary Clinton

"Why would you want to put people in charge of government who just don't want to do it? I mean, you wouldn't expect to see Al Qaeda members as pilots."

—former Rep. Alan Grayson (D-FL), on the prospects of Republicans taking back control of Congress in 2010

"That [Rick] Scott down there that's running for governor of Florida. Instead of running for governor of Florida, they ought to have him and shoot him. Put him against the wall and shoot him. He stole billions of dollars from the United States government and he's running for governor of Florida. He's a millionaire and a billionaire. He's no hero. He's a damn crook. It's just we don't prosecute big crooks."

—former Rep. Paul Kanjorski (D-PA), who, three months after making those remarks, wrote an op-ed in the *New York Times* calling for "civility and respect" in American political discourse

"How about just tracking down every single person who said, 'drill, baby, drill,' and putting them all in prison. Why don't we do that? Starting with Michael Steele."

—former Rep. Alan Grayson (D-FL)

"You think you are big enough to make me, you little wimp? Come on, come over here and make me, I dare you...You little fruitcake. You little fruitcake. I said you are a fruitcake."

—former Rep. Peter Stark (D-CA),
after former Rep. Scott McInnis (R-CO) told
him to "shut up" amid a legislative dispute

"You ever watch that TV series *Mad Men*? ... If I keep watching this program, will I ever find a happy person? Great television. Good drama. But a lot of really painful reminders in that show about how black people were supposed to run the elevators...were supposed to ask permission before they get on an elevator. The way women were treated is appalling, and only occasionally funny to me."

—Bill Clinton

"You know, education—if you make the most of it—you study hard, you do your homework, and you make an effort to be smart, you can do well. If you don't, you get stuck in Iraq."

—Sen. John Kerry (D-MA), botching a joke about
President Bush getting us stuck in Iraq

"If I could be the condom queen and get every young person in the United States who is engaging in sex to use a condom, I would wear a crown on my head with a condom on it."

—Jocelyn Elders, U.S. Surgeon General
under Bill Clinton

"I want you to disregard all the opposing counsel has said. I think they're delusionary. I think they've had something funny for lunch in their meal. I think they should be handcuffed, chained to a fence, and flogged, and all of their hearsay evidence should be thrown the hell out. And if they lie again, I'm going to go over there and kick them in the crotch. Thank you very much."

—former Rep. James Traficant (D-OH), during his
expulsion hearing from Congress for taking bribes
and kickbacks (he later served jail time)

"For the first time in my adult lifetime, I am really proud of my country. And not just because Barack has done well, but because I think people are hungry for change."

—Michelle Obama, campaigning for her husband in 2008

"God bless the America we are trying to create."

—Hillary Clinton

Crazy Quotes by Celebrity Nut Jobs and Media Blowhards

"I propose a limitation be put on how many squares of toilet paper can be used in any one sitting. Now, I don't want to rob any law-abiding American of his or her God-given rights, but I think we are an industrious enough people that we can make it work with only one square per restroom visit, except, of course, on those pesky occasions where two to three could be required."

—singer Sheryl Crow, on saving the planet

"They are possibly the dumbest people on the planet."

—Michael Moore, on his fellow Americans

"[Rush Limbaugh] just wants the country to fail. To me that's treason. He's not saying anything different than what Osama Bin Laden is saying. You might want to look into this, sir, because I think Rush Limbaugh was the twentieth hijacker but he was just so strung out on Oxycontin he missed his flight...Rush Limbaugh, I hope the country fails, I hope his kidneys fail, how about that? He needs a good waterboarding, that's what he needs."

—comedian Wanda Sykes at the 2009 White House Correspondents' Association dinner

"Isn't it a little racist to call it Black Friday?"

—talk show host Joy Behar

"I have to tell you, you know, it's part of reporting this case, this election, the feeling most people get when they hear Barack Obama's speech. My, I felt this thrill going up my leg."

—MSNBC's Chris Matthews

"Does [Fred Thompson] have sex appeal?…Can you smell the English Leather on this guy, the Aqua Velva, the sort of mature man's shaving cream, or whatever, you know, after he shaved? Do you smell that sort of—a little bit of cigar smoke?"

—Chris Matthews, on actor and former senator Fred Thompson

"Don't fear the terrorists. They're mothers and fathers."

—Rosie O'Donnell

"There is no terrorist threat. Yes, there have been horrific acts of terrorism and, yes, there will be acts of terrorism again. But that doesn't mean that there's some kind of massive terrorist threat."

—Michael Moore

"I feel like we have a very vagina-friendly administration."

—actress Rosario Dawson on the Obama administration

"We have a voice now, and we're not using it, and women have so much to lose. I mean, we could lose the right to our bodies…If you think that rape should be legal, then don't vote."

—actress Cameron Diaz

"Al Qaeda really hurt us, but not as much as Rupert Murdoch has hurt us, particularly in the case of Fox News. Fox News is worse than Al Qaeda—worse for our society. It's as dangerous as the Ku Klux Klan ever was."

—Keith Olbermann,
formerly of MSNBC, now on Current TV

"If I lived in Massachusetts, I'd try to vote ten times…Yeah that's right, I'd cheat to keep these bastards out. I would. Because that's exactly what they are."

—MSNBC's Ed Schultz

"We are pretty sure that we got Sarah Palin to do a guest spot on Glee. She'll be singing an original tune that I penned; it's called 'Look at Me, I'm Batshit Crazy.'"

—actress Jane Lynch

"Now let me tell you something about Sarah Palin, man: she's good masturbation material. The glasses and all that? Great masturbation material."

—actor Tracy Morgan, in a live interview on *Inside the NBA* on TNT, talking with Charles Barkley about an argument they have "all the time": Tina Fey or Sarah Palin?

"I take a three-minute shower. I even—brush my teeth while in the shower."

—actress Jennifer Aniston, on saving the planet

"I do believe that it's the first time in history that fire has ever melted steel. I do believe that it defies physics that World Trade Center Tower 7—Building 7, which collapsed in on itself—it is impossible for a building to fall the way it fell without explosives being involved. World Trade Center 7. World Trade [Center] 1 and 2 got hit by planes—7, miraculously, the first time in history, steel was melted by fire. It is physically impossible."

—Rosie O'Donnell, talking 9/11 "Trutherism"

"Do you think this Constitution-loving is getting out of hand?"

—talk show host Joy Behar

"Dick Cheney's heart's a political football. We ought to rip it out and kick it around and stuff it back in him."

—MSNBC's Ed Schultz

"America has been killing people on this continent since it was started. This country is not worth dying for."

—anti-war activist Cindy Sheehan

"I think that people like the Howard Sterns, the Bill O'Reillys, and to a lesser degree the bin Ladens of the world are making a horrible contribution."

—Sean Penn

"A spoiled child (Bush) is telling us our Social Security isn't safe anymore, so he is going to fix it for us. Well, here's your answer, you ungrateful whelp: [sound of four gunshots being fired.] Just try it, you little bastard. [audio of gun being cocked]."

—talk show host Randi Rhodes

"It makes it very difficult to quit smoking under this administration."

—Sean Penn, blaming President Bush for his smoking habit

"The Iraqis who have risen up against the occupation are not 'insurgents' or 'terrorists' or 'The Enemy.' They are the REVOLUTION, the Minutemen, and their numbers will grow—and they will win."

—Michael Moore

After-words

> *"If you can't answer a man's argument, all is not lost; you can still call him vile names."*
>
> **—Elbert Hubbard**

When All Else Fails: 125,000 Ways to Insult Liberals

Can't persuade anyone to your way of thinking? Kill 'em with words instead. This handy chart contains 125,000 potential insults you can lob at liberals.

Choose a word from each column, string them together, and fire away at all the "unmedicated, park-occupying douche bags" or "traitorous, Prius-driving asshats" in your midst. Think of it as your very own Magic Hate Ball.

Column A	Column B	Column C
spineless	America-blaming	socialists
godless	Bible-bashing	elitists
uninformed	Jesus-trashing	crybabies
angry	tax-hiking	hypocrites
knee-jerk	terrorist-coddling	moonbats
irrational	pot-smoking	weasels
hysterical	tree-hugging	Marxists
unmedicated	God-hating	douche bags
obnoxious	liberal-media-parroting	crackpots
pathetic	troop-slandering	sodomites
whiny	flag-burning	degenerates
amoral	body-piercing	lunatics
miserable	capitalism-bashing	invertebrates
naïve	drum-circling	Commies
unpatriotic	park-occupying	hippies
unhinged	MSNBC-worshipping	sissies
deranged	compost-piling	vegans
brainless	ACLU-loving	crackheads
incoherent	bailout-cheering	wackos
un-American	sushi-eating	dumbocrats
insane	nose-piercing	heathens

Column A	Column B	Column C
pompous	gay-marrying	morons
arrogant	freedom-hating	demonrats
clueless	tofu-licking	deadbeats
ignorant	latte-drinking	loons
unwashed	granny-euthanizing	parasites
screeching	wealth-redistributing	twits
sanctimonious	liberty-loathing	fruitcakes
delusional	granola-munching	pinheads
unsaved	gun-grabbing	infidels
pinko	criminal-coddling	weenies
wimpy	welfare-depending	deviants
flaming	arugula-eating	hoodlums
cowardly	Birkenstock-wearing	hedonists
shrill	Prius-driving	wusses
lobotomized	patchouli-slathering	cretins
lazy	bongo-playing	fools
crazy	naked yoga-ing	envirofreaks
crunchy	dreadlock-wearing	peaceniks
tie-dyed	Marx-loving	fornicators
traitorous	jihad-joining	stoners
unemployed	Constitution-shredding	pagans

Column A	Column B	Column C
flaky	victim-playing	pacifists
unshaven	cannabis-cultivating	eunuchs
neurotic	stem-cell-sucking	asshats
dimwitted	bong-smoking	Christophobes
hairy	commune-dwelling	libtards
smelly	Woodstock-reenacting	bedwetters
smug	free-market-fearing	bottom-feeders
hemp-clad	condom-dispensing	ecoweenies

Acknowledgments

This book would not have been necessary if it hadn't been for the politicians on both sides who have worked so diligently to divide the country. Nor would it have been possible—or at least not as much fun to write—without the inspiration provided by comedians like Jon Stewart and Stephen Colbert, who put politics in perspective and help dull the pain.

I am indebted to my editor, Shana Drehs, and to Deb Werksman, Sean Murray, and the staff at Sourcebooks, whose hard work and enthusiasm made this book a reality, and to Barret Neville, whose editorial guidance and vision helped shape this project.

Many thanks to Thomas Fahy, who offered indispensable feedback, careful editing, and unflagging support from the beginning; to Lee Levine, Warren Graff, and Mitch Cox, whose considerable comedic talents greatly enhanced many parts of this book; as well as to Lou Kipilman, Danielle Svetcov, Todd Smithline, Max Zarzana, John Nein, Joshua Swartz, Josh Archibald,

Daniel Wasson, and Sarah Schroeder—all of whom provided valuable assistance and shrewd insights during many stages of the writing process.

My family provided not only inspiration but, somewhat inadvertently, much of the field research that helped inform this book. I am grateful for the love and support of my parents, Ken and Caryl, who taught me the value of tolerance and spirited debate, and my brother, Todd, who taught me the importance of defending my position, especially while being hunted with a BB gun. To the DeCastros, a special salute to Mike for embracing his designation as "Uncle Blowhard" with a passion, Lois for her creative inspiration, and Baylee for living the liberal dream. To Jessica and Chris Swanson, Patty, Neil, and the entire Smithline clan, thank you for your loving encouragement and the lively conversations.

I am also endlessly grateful to many friends for their unfailing support: Marty Chester, Dave Uram, Alison Tshangana, David Ziring, Jodi and Andy Brown, Aviva Rosenthal, Liana Schwarz, Alex Kazan, Shannon Farley, Lesley Reidy, Kim Neumann, Lara Abbott, Rebecca Davis, Melody King, Bridgette Bates, Tatyana Tsinberg, Carol Brydolf, the Suffin family, and the numerous other family members and friends who took time to share their political wisdom and partisan horror stories.

I'd also like to acknowledge several important influences who shaped my political and humor sensibilities: Matt Dorf, my former bureau chief, who schooled me in the ways of Washington; Donal Brown, my high school journalism teacher, who showed me how to kill 'em with words; Dave Kreines, a master of both words and wit, and one of the best friends I ever knew; and the late Duane Garrett, one of the funniest commentators and most brilliant political minds of his generation.

And most importantly, I am grateful beyond words to my son, Joel, for helpfully trying to edit drafts of this book in crayon and for laughing at all my jokes; and to my wife, Laura, who inspires me every day. Her abiding faith, brilliant insights, and sharp editing helped make every part of this book better. Together, their love and laughter make every part of life better, too.

About the Author

D aniel Kurtzman chronicles the absurdities of politics as editor of politicalhumor.about .com, the popular website that is part of The New York Times Company's About.com network. As a former Washington correspondent-turned-political satirist, his work has appeared in the *New York Times*, the *Huffington Post*, the *San Francisco Chronicle*, and the *Funny Times*, among other publications. He lives with his wife and their son in the San Francisco Bay Area. An equal opportunity offender, Kurtzman is also the author of *How to Win a Fight with a Conservative*.

www.FightLiberals.com

Facebook: facebook.com/politicalhumor

Twitter: twitter.com/politicalhumor